KENT'S MILITARY HERITAGE

Dean Hollands

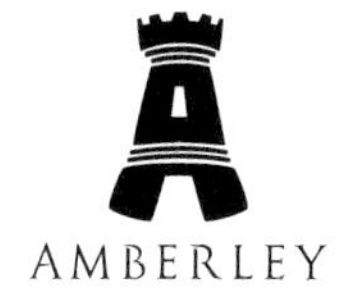

This book is dedicated to the memory of all those whose actions and deeds have resulted in the creation of Kent's military heritage, be they human or animal, and to those who work tirelessly towards its preservation.

First published 2020

Amberley Publishing
The Hill, Stroud
Gloucestershire, GL5 4EP

www.amberley-books.com

Logo source material courtesy of Gerry van Tonder

ISBN 978 1 4456 9095 7 (print)
ISBN 978 1 4456 9096 4 (ebook)

British Library Cataloguing in Publication Data.
A catalogue record for this book is available from the British Library.

Typesetting by Aura Technology and Software Services, India. Printed in Great Britain.

Contents

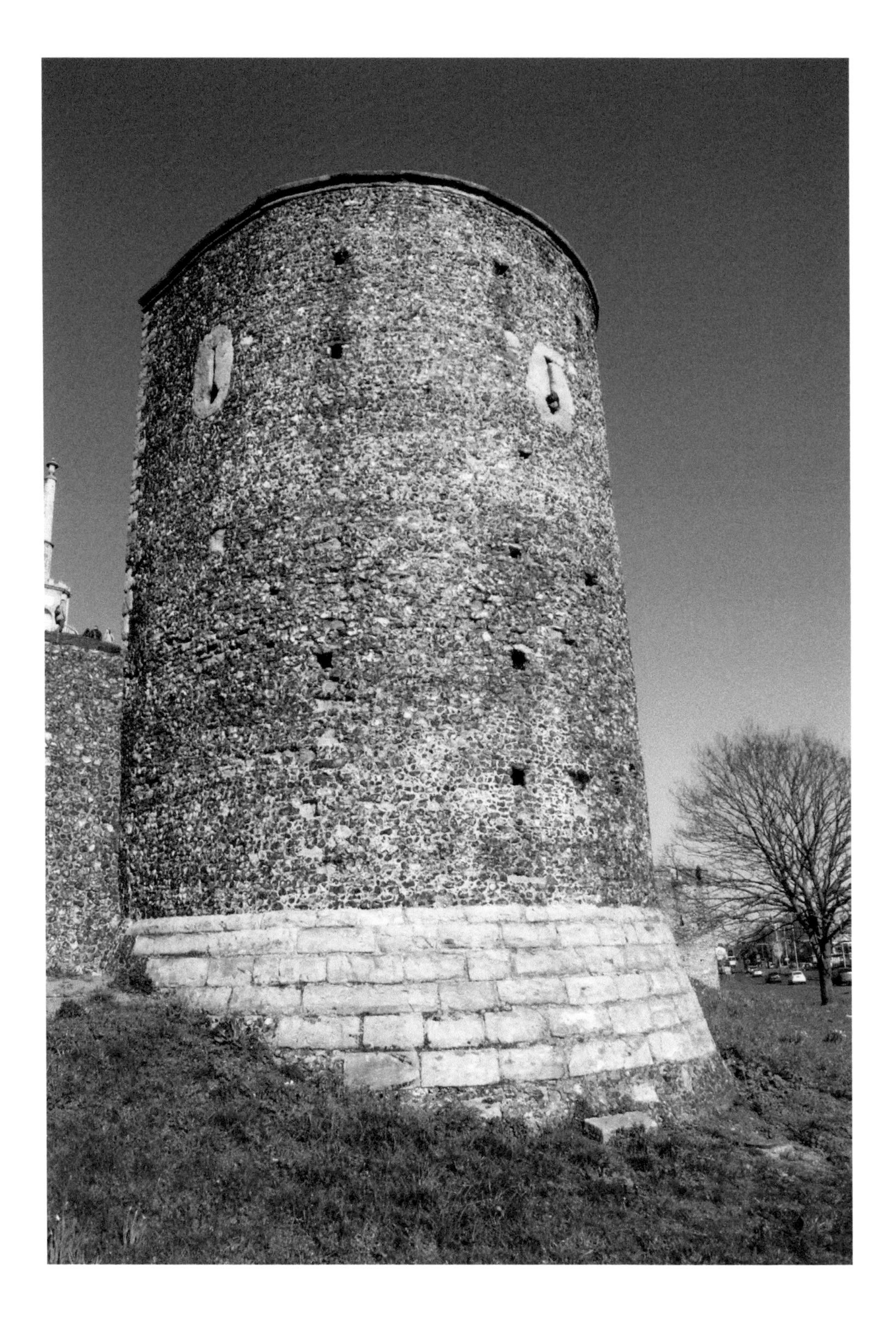

Introduction

Kent, 'The Garden of England', is a county blessed with a beauty and abundance of military heritage as diverse as it is ancient; a heritage that during its darkest days experienced the bloodthirsty wrath of raiders and invaders intent on murder, massacre, invasion, conquest and subjugation. However, despite the passage of time, many of the scars, remnants and reminders of those pugilistic struggles and epic military encounters remain today for all to see. In all their forms, these cultural assets serve as a poignant legacy to the courage, unyielding determination, and sacrifices made by the people and animals of Kent who have gallantly served their county and country in equal measure. From its Iron Age hill forts and Norman castles to its prehistoric monuments, and modern museums and memorials, Kent's landscape harbours some of the most unique and interesting military heritage to be found anywhere in the country.

While the militia and regular military units of Kent have for centuries answered the call to arms at home and abroad, its coastal defences have resolutely defended the county and nation, adapting to new threats, new technologies, and new enemies. During the twentieth and twenty-first centuries its airfields have defended the nation's airspace and provided support for ground force operations around the world in the war against tyranny and terrorism, and, for many centuries, its dockyards have played a pivotal role defending the peoples and interests of Britain's Empire.

Such is the extensive and diverse nature of Kent's military heritage it is not possible to comment on any aspect of that heritage in depth within the pages of this publication. However, this book does provide a concise and informative overview of the important military periods in the county's history, as well as insights into some of the many people, places and events that have contributed to its remarkable military legacy. In so doing, this book signposts readers to the key heritage attractions and locations within the county. It is the author's hope that readers will be inspired and intrigued by its contents to learn more about the county's military heritage, to visit the many wonderful attractions and sites it has to offer and to share that experience with others.

Dean Hollands, 2019

1. Invaders and Raiders

In 6000 BC the land mass connecting Britain to Europe collapsed. Now an island, Britain was cut off and isolated and in time, stories circulated of mythical creatures and demonic gods living in a land of fabulous wealth and riches beyond imagination. For those courageous enough to undertake the perilous crossing, seemingly endless chances for status, power and glory awaited them. Being the closest point to Europe, Kent became the landing point for explorers, invaders, raiders and traders into this new land of opportunity.

Tantalised by such tales, a few brave explorers made the dangerous crossing to Kent's shores. News spread of their voyages and the bountiful resources and riches they had discovered. Owing to its short distance (21 miles) from France, Kent became the gateway for successive invasions of settlers in search of a better life and by traders keen to exploit commercial opportunities. Military forces soon followed, small marauding groups sporadically attacked settlements in search of plunder, while larger well-organised armies arrived intent on conquest, occupation and subjugation.

The first major invasion of Kent took place in August 55 BC, commanded by Julius Caesar. The focus of Caesar's invasion was to prevent continued support of rebels in Gaul from tribes in Britain, to find friendly tribes to trade with and to secure new allies.

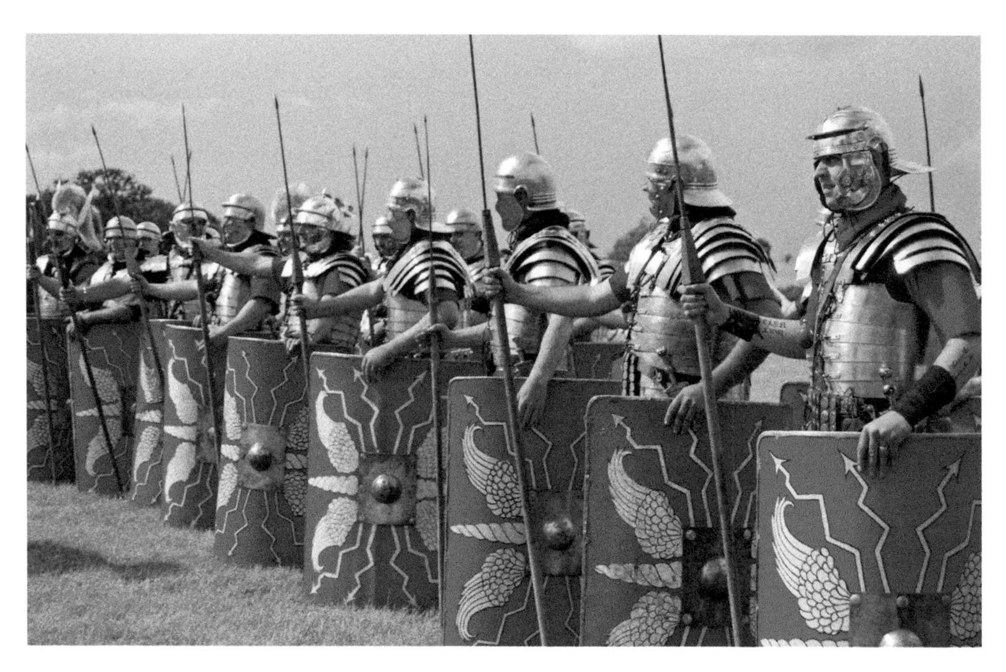

Roman re-enactors at Dover.

A small Roman task force of eighty ships conveyed 12,000 men and an assortment of cavalry to Pegwell Bay. There they were met by the Cantiaci tribe from Cantium (Kent). As the legionnaires waded ashore burdened with weapons and equipment, they were easy targets for the tribesmen's javelins and slingshot. As soldiers emerged onto the beach, savage fighting took place, with the Cantiaci riding horses and driving chariots into them. Eventually the legionnaires organised themselves, forcing the Britons off the beach and back inland.

Seeking a peace treaty, the routed Britons sent envoys to Caesar, but he took them hostage. Four days after landing, a ferocious storm and high tides drove Caesar's fleet onto the beach. While the Romans repaired their ships, the Cantiaci tribe once more mustered their forces to attack. Low on food, Caesar sent men inland to gather supplies, but the Britons ambushed them. Caesar eventually engaged them in battle on open ground. The undisciplined tactics of the barbarian army were no match for the disciplined manoeuvres of the Romans. Defeated, the humiliated Britons suffered heavy casualties; Caesar, now triumphant, returned to Gaul.

The following year, Caesar returned with an invasion force of 800 ships, 25,000 soldiers and 2,000 cavalrymen. It was the largest amphibious operation in history, unsurpassed until the allied invasion of Normandy in 1944. Within three months Caesar had gained a decisive victory that allowed him to secure peace in the region and once more return to Gaul triumphant, although almost a hundred years would pass before the Romans would conquer Britain.

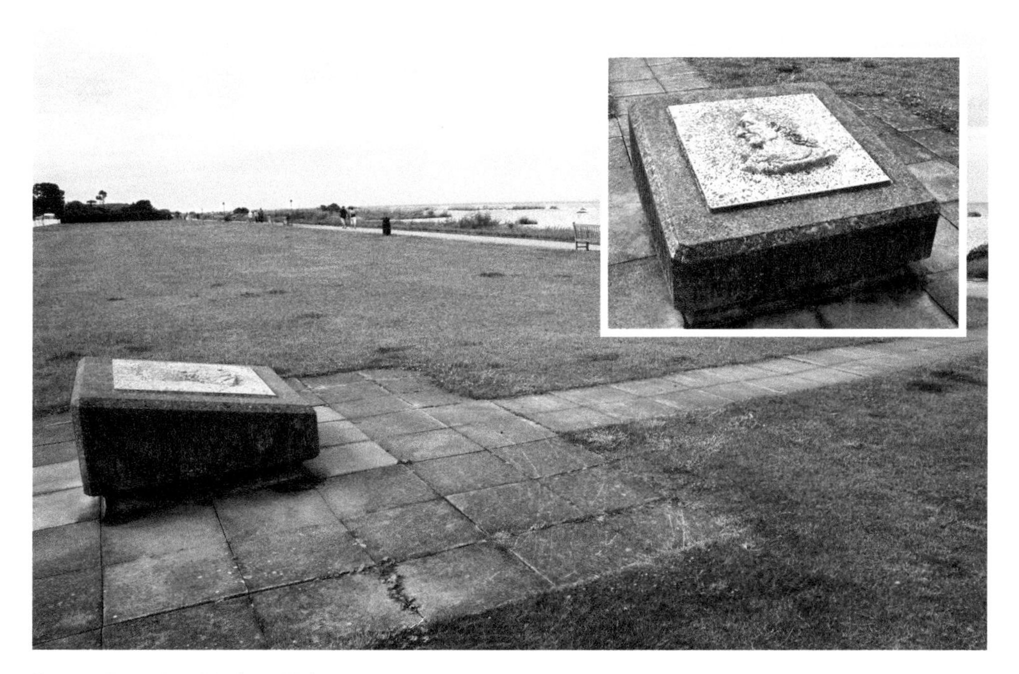

Roman Invasion Marker, Walmer.

Inset: Roman Invasion Marker.

In AD 43, King Verica, who'd been ousted from Atrebates (Sussex) by King Caractacus, of the Catuvellauni tribe, petitioned Emperor Claudius for help to regain his kingdom. Claudius responded, landing an army of 35,000 seasoned legionnaires under the command of General Aulus Plautius Silvanus at Richborough. There he faced an enemy of 20,000 Cantiaci warriors supported by a powerful coalition of tribes from the north of the Thames. Commanded by King Caractacus and his brother Togodumnus, the coalition comprised 70,000 Catuvellauni tribesmen, 40,000 men from the Trinovantes tribe in Essex and 40,000 warriors from smaller tribes across Britain.

Silvanus marched his army from Richborough to capture the Cantiaci capital, Canterbury. Then, intent on crushing the Catuvellauni army, he marched his forces across the North Downs towards the River Thames. Caractacus, joined by reinforcements from Togodumnus, assembled his army on the west bank of the River Medway and planned to halt the advancing Romans at a crossing point near Burnham Court.

With both forces encamped on either side of the river, the Romans seized the initiative with a surprise attack, 'The Battle of Medway'. A detachment of Roman auxiliaries swam across the Medway slaughtering and immobilising most of the Britons' horses. During the ensuing panic, General Vespasian (future Emperor of Rome) attempted to secure victory by making a surprise crossing of the river. Both sides fought a fierce and bloody engagement, and by nightfall there was no conclusive outcome. The following day, General Gnaeus Hosidius Geta attempted to outflank the Britons and was almost killed. His attack caused Caractacus's force to retreat, securing a Roman victory. Despite heavy casualties, the Britons refused to accept defeat and headed for the River Thames where they joined Togodumnus and the rest of his coalition forces.

Following the Romans' arrival, further battles took place during which Togodumnus was defeated and fatally wounded. This victory and the defeat of the Cantiaci gained the Romans a strong foothold in Britain and by AD 47 southern Britain was part of the Roman Empire (although Britain would not be conquered until AD 77.) Today a large stone of remembrance marks the location of the Battle of Medway in AD 43 and commemorates the Roman army's defeat of Caractacus and the British tribes under his command.

The Romans left Britain in AD 410, leaving it once more to the ravages of internal politics and the focus of invaders. It wasn't long before another plea for help led to invasion, when in AD 449, 300 Angle, Saxon and Jute mercenaries led by brothers Hengist and Horsa landed at Ebbsfleet. King Vortigern had requested their help to repel attacks from invading Picts and Scots. In return, Vortigern promised money and the Isle of Thanet as a reward. Having beaten the invaders, Hengist and Horsa lived peacefully for a while until Vortigern stopped supplies of gold and silver due to them. Their response was to denounce the worthiness of the Britons and exalt the value of their land to encourage others in Germania to join them in an attack. Thousands answered the call; they slaughtered thousands, ransacked cities and looted villas across the country before Hengist and Horsa returned to Kent to declare themselves independent leaders.

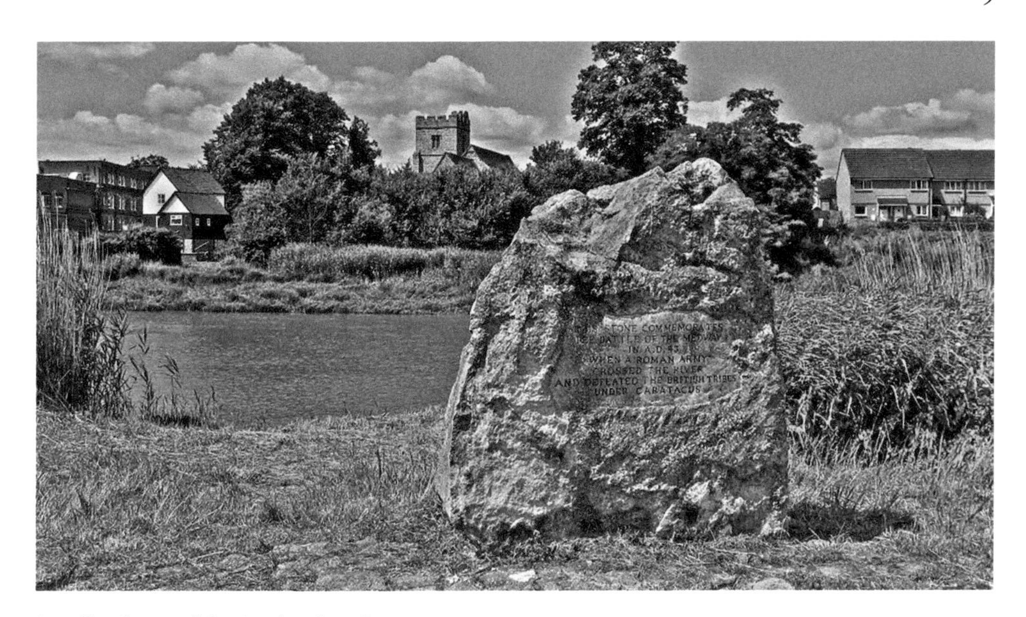

Snodland, site of the Battle of Medway, AD 43.

In AD 455 Vortigern sent a huge army command by his sons, Vortimer and Catigern, to invade Kent. After they crossed the River Medway at Aylesford, a decisive battle took place, during which Horsa and Catigern were killed. Vortigern's army was driven back over the river by Hengist. Hengist drove Vortimer out of Kent in AD 456, annihilating his army at Crayford, Dartford. Today the remains of two Neolithic chamber tombs, Kit's Coty House and the White Horse Stone, mark the alleged burial places of Catigern and Horsa. Victory at this battle led to the Anglo-Saxons ruling Britain and dividing the land into seven kingdoms.

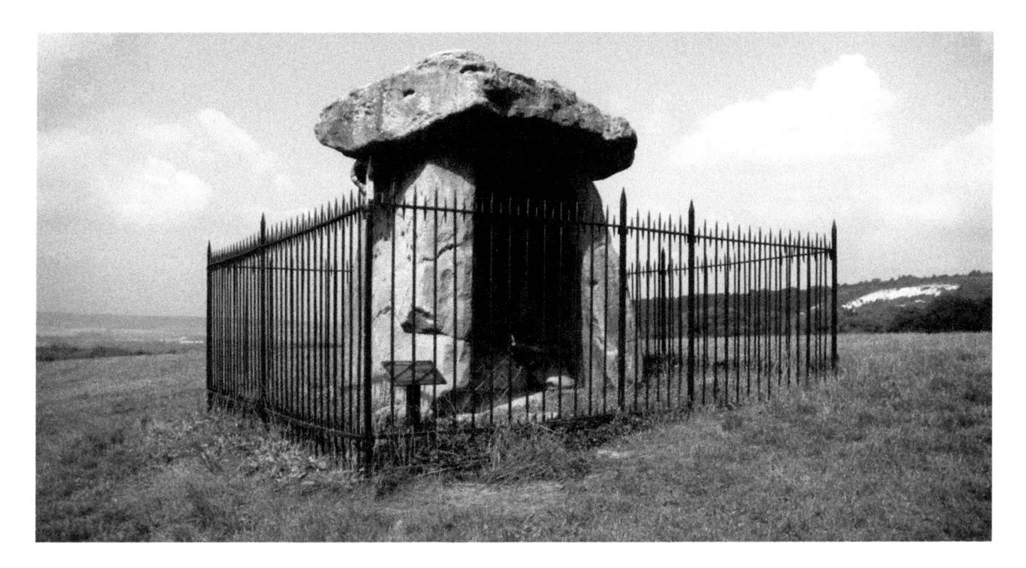

Remains of Catigern's burial tomb, Maidstone.

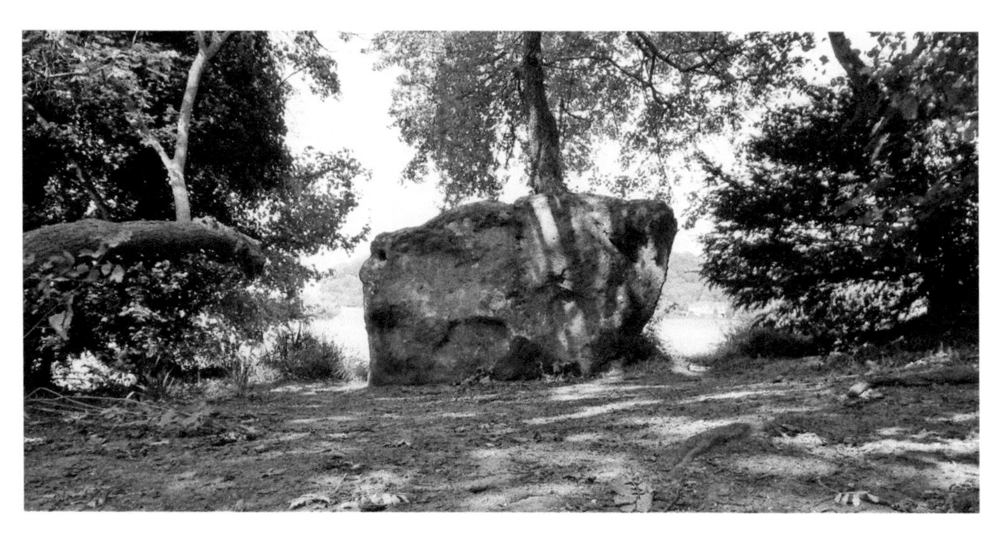

Remains of Horsa's burial tomb, Maidstone.

During the late eighth century, Kent was again invaded. This time it was the turn of the Vikings of Norway, Sweden and Denmark. After raiding communities along Kent's coast, they moved further inland. The *Anglo-Saxon Chronicles* shows that in 804, the nuns of Lyminge sought refuge in Canterbury to escape them. For decades Vikings slaughtered and plundered their way across the county, battling and skirmishing against Kentish forces, during which they repeatedly targeted key towns and cities such as Canterbury and Rochester.

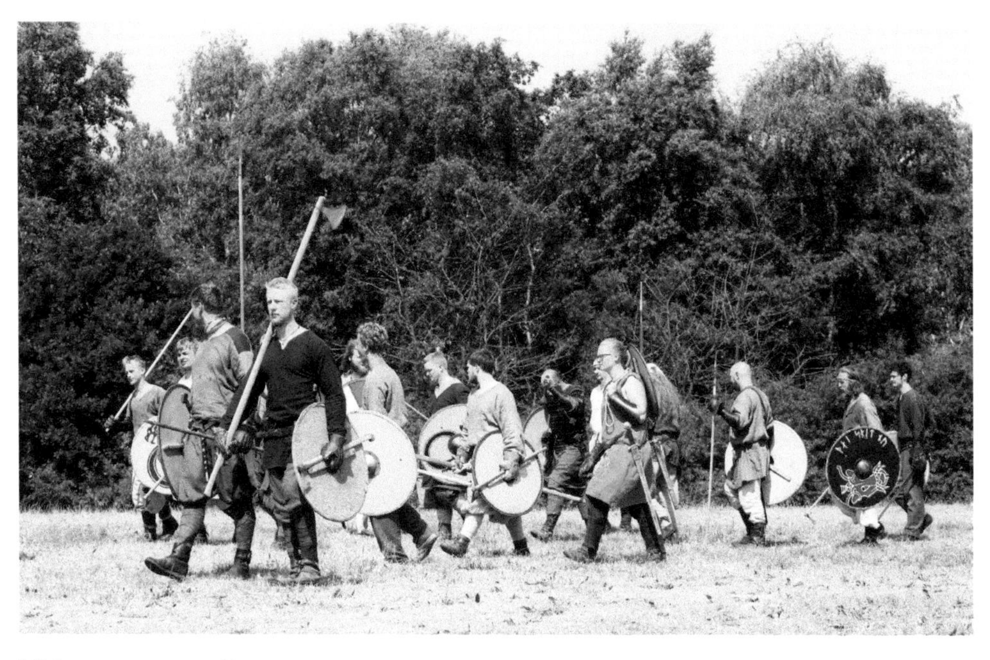

Viking re-enactors at Ramsgate.

Between 851–55 Vikings built fortifications on the isles of Thanet and Sheppey where they overwintered their armies. Apart from a few periods of agreed settlement, their reign of terror continued for a further 200 years, as successive armies pillaged their way through Kent, raiding, plundering and searching for new and fertile land. On the clifftop at Pegwell Bay, Ramsgate, is 'The Hugin', a replica of Viking longship that sailed from Denmark to Kent in 1949 to mark the 1,500th anniversary of their first invasion of Kent. The Viking occupation of Britain ended with the Norman Conquest of 1066 by William, Duke of Normandy; this would not be the last invasion of Britain, but it was the last time it was conquered.

William's victory over King Harold, known today as the Battle of Hastings, was just the opening engagement of a long and bloody process of occupation, subjugation and conquest. In the weeks that followed, he unveiled his template for conquest in Kent. He razed entire villages using a scorched earth policy against anyone who rebelled, put inhabitants to the sword, slaughtered livestock, and destroyed food stores. Residents of Romney, having attacked and killed a force of his men who'd mistakenly landed there, were the first to experience his wrath.

To prevent further uprisings along the coast, William marched his army to Dover where having learned of Romney's fate, the town surrendered. William's next target was Canterbury and Rochester, who also surrendered. While en route to London, he sent troops to Winchester to take control of the royal treasury and confirm the surrender of Queen Edith, Edward the Confessor's widow. In London William was crowned King of England on Christmas Day 1066, and in time became better known as 'William the Conqueror'. The aftermath of the invasion

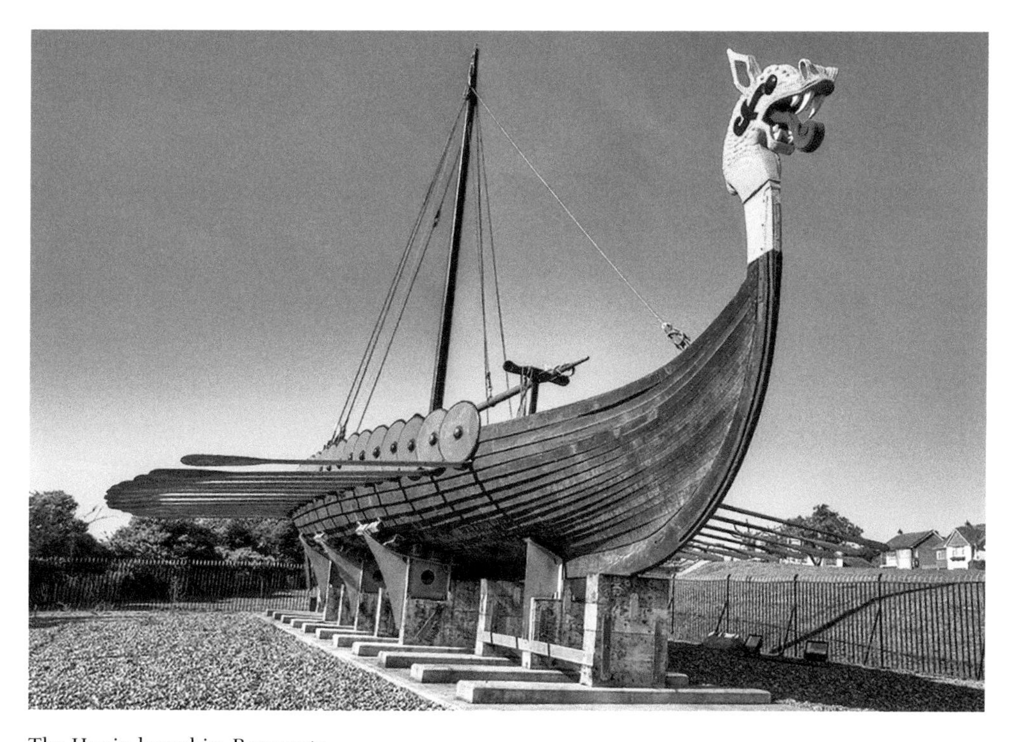

The Hugin longship, Ramsgate.

was bloody, brutal and protracted, forever changing the traditional Saxon way of life. Having conquered England, William and his heirs faced protracted attacks along the Kent coast from raiders and invaders intent on plundering and conquering England.

Despite such threats, England remained invasion free until the reign of King John. It was John's brutal regime and notorious habit of extracting monies from his subjects that resulted in Prince Louis (later King Louis VIII) of France invading Kentish soil. In 1208, John imposed enormous taxes on his barons and tried to confiscate all church property. To ensure cooperation he ordered both to give him hostages, which caused him to be hated by the church and barons. In 1215 they imposed Magna Carta, a charter which included a 'security clause' allowing them to wage war against him if he did not comply. Although the king signed the charter, he at once sought papal support to revoke it.

As a result, many barons withdrew their loyalty to King John, and invited Prince Louis of France, grandson of Henry II, to invade England and take the throne. On 21 May 1216, Louis's army landed at Sandwich and marched on London. John retreated west and Louis, having entered the capital and been proclaimed king, started his campaign to oust his rival. Conflict erupted and by the summer of 1216, Louis had overrun Kent and much of southern England, capturing Rochester Castle and besieging Dover Castle. Notwithstanding bitter resistance and several months of stand-offs, on 14 October he was compelled to make a truce before carrying war to other parts of the country. Following King John's death during the night of 18–19 October 1216, his nine-year-old son Henry III became king and was crowned on 28 October. The barons rejected Louis in favour of Henry and following several battles throughout the land, Louis was beaten at Lincoln and returned to France, leaving Henry III to rule England.

Kent's next invasion was a minor and short-lived affair, led by the Belgium-born Perkin Warbeck. The son of a Tournai boatman, Warbeck was carefully tutored to impersonate Richard, Duke of York, son of Edward IV and a legitimate heir to the throne of England, who was imprisoned in the Tower of London with his brother (Princes in the Tower) and had disappeared. On this pretext, Warbeck obtained support from the French Court, Burgundy and other European Courts for his claim to the throne. His first attempted invasion occurred at Deal in 1495, arriving with fourteen ships and several thousand men. Before launching a full-scale invasion, he took a small force of 150 men ashore to see whether he could gather further support. The Sheriff of Kent attacked and, before Warbeck had even disembarked, they had slain most of his men, forcing him to retreat.

Influenced by mercantilism and embroiled in centuries of conflict over fishing, trading routes and colonies, Dutch and English forces clashed over control of the seas, and war was inevitable. The Medway was once again the location of a great battle. In June 1667, the Dutch fleet, under the command of Lieutenant Admiral Michiel de Ruyter, launched an audacious raid against England, targeting the dockyard at Chatham. Lasting six days, the attack resulted in the Dutch fleet capturing the fort at Sheerness and its surrounding areas. The Dutch fleet smashed through the huge defensive chain spanning the Medway between Gillingham and Hoo Ness and, capturing the batteries at each end, they continued inland towards Chatham.

During the attack the Dutch captured several ships, including the English flagship the *Royal Charles*, and set many others alight. With the Medway engulfed in flames, the Royal Navy sank and grounded several of its largest vessels to prevent further ships being captured. The garrison at Upnor Castle used heavy guns to force the Dutch back along the river and out to sea with their valuable prizes. It was a huge and humiliating defeat for the navy that caused many to fear it was the start of a mainland invasion by Dutch forces.

To end Britain's involvement in the Seven Years War of 1756–63, the French planned to land 100,000 soldiers in Britain, but several heavy defeats weakened their navy and plans to invade were abandoned in 1763 and similarly to plans in 1770, 1779 and 1803. French invasion fears remained real until the end of the Napoleonic Wars in 1815, as, while victorious Britain rested on its laurels, the French embraced advances in technology. Combining steam power and developments in ship design, they constructed iron-clad ships fitted with new riffled artillery capable of firing 8,000 yards (7315m, twice that of existing guns), gaining naval superiority. Despite their supremacy, fears of an invasion by the old enemy never materialised. Britain would however fear invasion and be the object of invasion plans and attacks from new enemies.

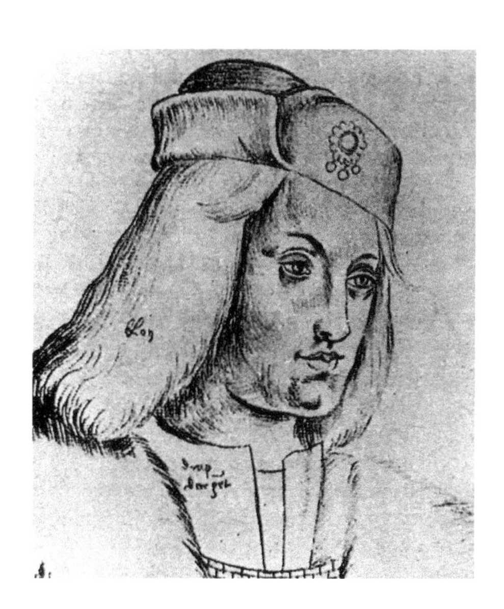

Right: The imposter, Perkin Warbeck.

Below: Depiction of the Battle of Medway, 1667.

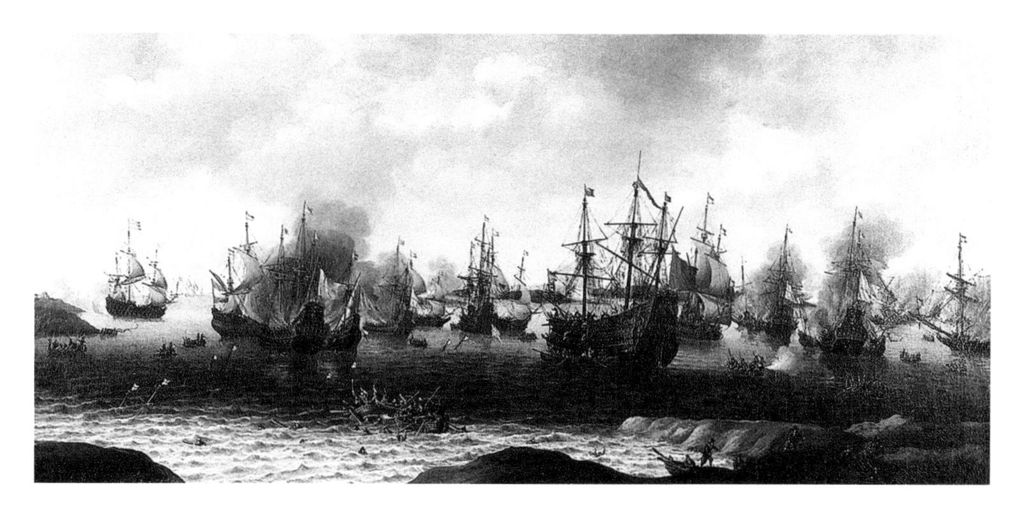

2. Early Defences: Celtic Hill Forts to Norman Castles

The Cantiaci, Celtic people from Gaul and Flanders, emigrated to Kent during the Iron Age, around 500 BC. Having integrated with local tribes, they established settlements with defences against their rivals. They built the first fortifications on hilltops, basic single bank and shallow ditch earthworks, topped by a simple palisade that enclosed large areas and followed the natural contours of the hill.

Building ports at Dubris (Dover) and Lemanis (Lympne), the Cantiaci developed important trade links with the Continent and Middle East. But they faced continual threats from the expanding Roman Empire and barbarian tribes in search of new lands. During the early part of 100 BC, the Belgae arrived from northern Gaul in such numbers that the Cantiaci rebuilt and re-enforced their existing forts and constructed new ones. These had more complex defences using two or three lines of earthworks to provide greater protection against invaders.

A great Iron Age hill fort once dominated the clifftop where Dover Castle now stands. Today little survives of this mighty structure; successive rebuilding has all but erased it from history. However, near the village of Ightham, on the summit of Oldbury hill amid a wooded plateau, are the remains of one of Britain's largest hill forts. Diamond in shape, it measures 4,429 feet (1,350 metres) from north to south and 2,296 feet (700 metres) east to west covering an area of around 120 acres. Around its north, west and south sides is a single bank and ditch, although in several places the bank is doubled to give extra defences. The bank rose to 33 feet (10 metres) with a V-shaped ditch around 5 feet (1.5 metres) deep.

Today the bank stands at 3 feet (1 metre), with a span of 11 feet (3.5 metres). Entrances were constructed on the north-east and southern ends of the fort. More banks protected the southern entrance, while a steep cliff edge protected the north-east side, and along the top of the hill ran a large wooden palisade. Partially excavated in 1938, and again in 1983/84, the archaeological evidence showed that the site was constructed rapidly, on an enormous scale, and never permanently occupied.

When Julius Caesar attacked the fort in 54 BC, his legionnaires faced a sustained barrage of stones, javelins and arrows. Unable to breach the walls, they used their shields as a protection to place bundles of wood at the northern entrance, then set it alight. When the gates were destroyed, the Romans entered and quickly captured the fort. Evidence of this fire was found during the 1938 excavation.

Constructed at the same time as Oldbury, the 26-acre site at Bigbury hill near Canterbury was located on high ground overlooking the River Stour. Built 200 feet (60 metres) above sea level, it stretches 1,000 feet (305 metres) east to west by 700 feet (213 metres) north to south and is enclosed by a 16-foot- (4.8-metre) wide perimeter ditch and earthwork bank. A solid timber palisade once surrounded the fort providing enhanced security

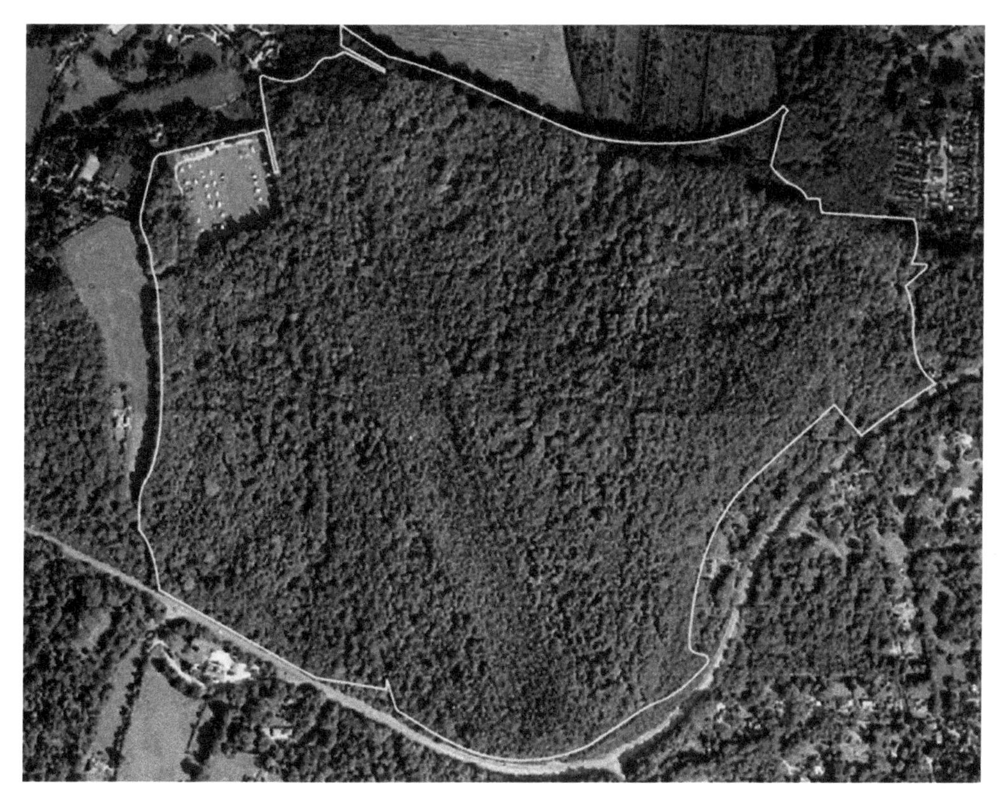

Aerial view of Oldbury Hill Fort. (PP.)

against attack. Following the contours of the hillside, its ramparts were irregular in shape. Excavations in the early 1960s showed the fort had two entrances, one on the east side and one on the west, each defended by a staggered fortification comprising two ditches and a bank.

Julius Caesar claimed Bigbury as the location of the first battle upon his return in 54 BC. In his account of the campaign he wrote:

> We marched by night for about 12 miles before coming in sight of the enemy forces. They had moved with their cavalry and chariots down from the higher ground to a river [the Stour] and were trying to engage us in battle. When our cavalry drove them back, they hid in the wood, where they enjoyed a position with good man-made defences because many trees had been cut down and used to block entrances to it. The Britons came out of the woods in small groups to fight. But the men of the Seventh Legion, holding up their shields to form a protective shell, piled up earth against the fortifications and captured the place.

While Iron Age defences were adequate for tribal warfare, they were no match for a direct assault by 5,000 organised, well-equipped battle-hardened Roman legionnaires. Like Oldbury, the Romans briefly used Bigbury as a military encampment. Both hill forts are accessible, and artefacts unearthed during their excavation can be seen at Canterbury Museum and Maidstone Museum. There exist the remains of other Iron Age forts across the county, but none are as outstanding as Oldbury.

Having invaded Kent in AD 43, Tiberius Claudius consolidated his position in the south by fortifying key townships such as Canterbury (Durovernum Cantiacorum), Rochester (Durobrivae) and Richborough (Rutupiae) against attack from Frankish and Saxon pirates. Known as Saxon Shore Forts, eleven were constructed along the south coast, four in Kent at Dover (Dubris), Lympne (Lemanis), Reculver (Regulbium) and Richborough (Rutupiae). The most symbolic of these is the one at Richborough, built on the site of the invasion beachhead of AD 43. It was also the location used for their departure in AD 410.

Richborough was an important port and supply depot; the original location contained a substantial system of defensive earthworks. During the second century, in response to threats from Saxon raiders along the south coast, the Romans erected massive 30-foot- (9-metre) high and 12-foot- (3.7-metre) wide stone walls, crowned with parapets and backed by an inner earth mound. They placed stone towers at intervals along the wall and at each corner of the fort. Outside the walls they dug a system of broad double ditches, making Richborough one of the most fortified military installations in south Britain. Today only the walls on three sides of the fort and the surrounding earthworks remain. Erected beside a natural harbour and surrounded by water on three sides, Richborough Fort offered an accessible landing place for trade and military use. Today centuries of erosion and silting have left it landlocked, 2 miles from the current foreshore. Preserved by Historic England, the site is open to the public and has a small informative museum.

With no thought to protecting their shoreline following the Romans' exodus in AD 410, Germanic settlers used stone from the shore forts to build churches, and the forts became derelict. It wasn't until Alfred the Great unified southern England that serious attention was given to repelling the raiders. Rather than defending the shoreline as the Romans had done, Alfred concentrated on building a few wooden forts at strategic locations

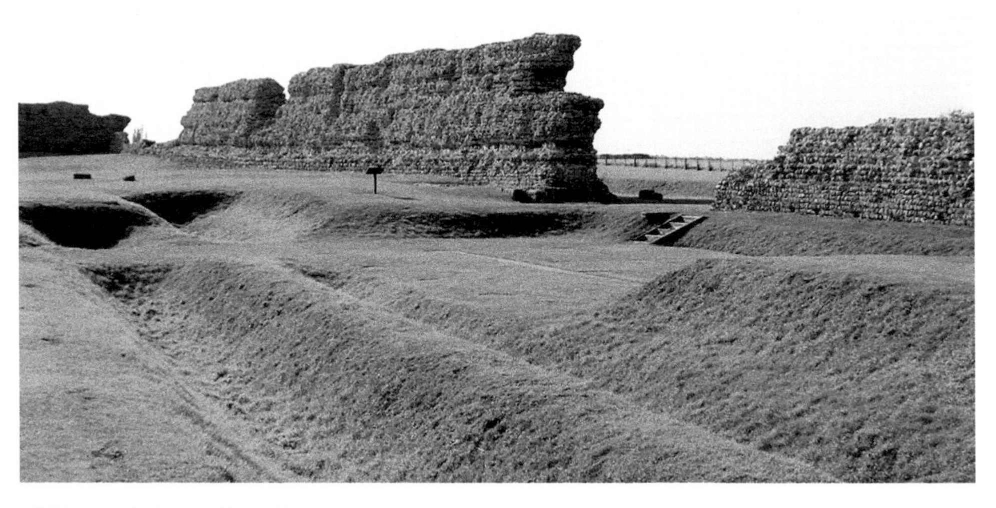

Richborough Saxon Shore Fort.

and improving existing fortifications in key towns such as Canterbury and Rochester. Consequently, he developed an integrated system of defences that included a series of fortified settlements known as burhs (defensive strongholds and muster points) connected by Roman roads and hilltop beacons. Some burhs were constructed from scratch by creating large encirclements of earth banks topped with wooden palisades, gates, towers, ditches and rows of fire-hardened stakes.

When hilltop beacons signalled danger, the roads enabled movement at speed either towards the safety of the burhs or from the burh to engage the enemy. Of the thirty-three burhs built by Alfred, only one was sited in Kent, at Newenden (Eorpeburnan). Erected on new foundations it comprised a 20-acre enclosure defended on three sides by a broad bank and ditch, and on the fourth by marshland. Although no visible evidence of the burh exists today, there are earthwork remains of a medieval fort, and Castle Toll, an early Norman castle, can still be seen.

The Normans were master castle builders who, following their invasion in 1066, built temporary fortifications, motte-and-bailey structures, to increase control over the people of England and to defend their new lands against rebellion and invasion. Incorporating the ancient Celtic and Roman defensive concepts of ditches, ramparts and walls, the Normans added a large conical-shaped earthen mound (the motte). These were often 100 feet (30 metres) high with a diameter of 300 feet (90 metres). Built on pre-existing features such as hills or artificial mounds created by piling up earth, the tops were flattened, a wooden keep added, and a large ditch dug around the base. The motte overlooked a large enclosed courtyard (the bailey) and tall wooden fencing and water-filled ditches surrounded the base. The bailey housed halls, kitchens, stores, stables, chapel, barracks, and workshops. A wooden bridge that could be raised when needed connected the motte to the bailey.

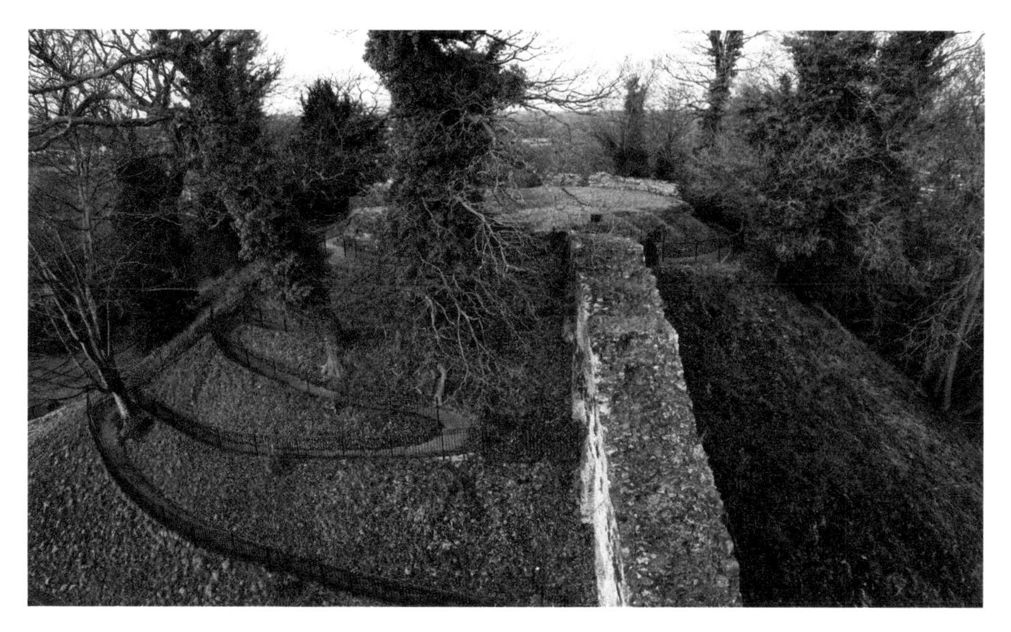

Tonbridge Castle's motte.

The Normans were also great architects and soon replaced their wooden castles with stone ones, such as those at Tonbridge, Canterbury, Cooling and Allington. Others like Binbury, Kent's earliest motte-and-bailey castle, and Thurnham, replaced only their keeps with stone ones.

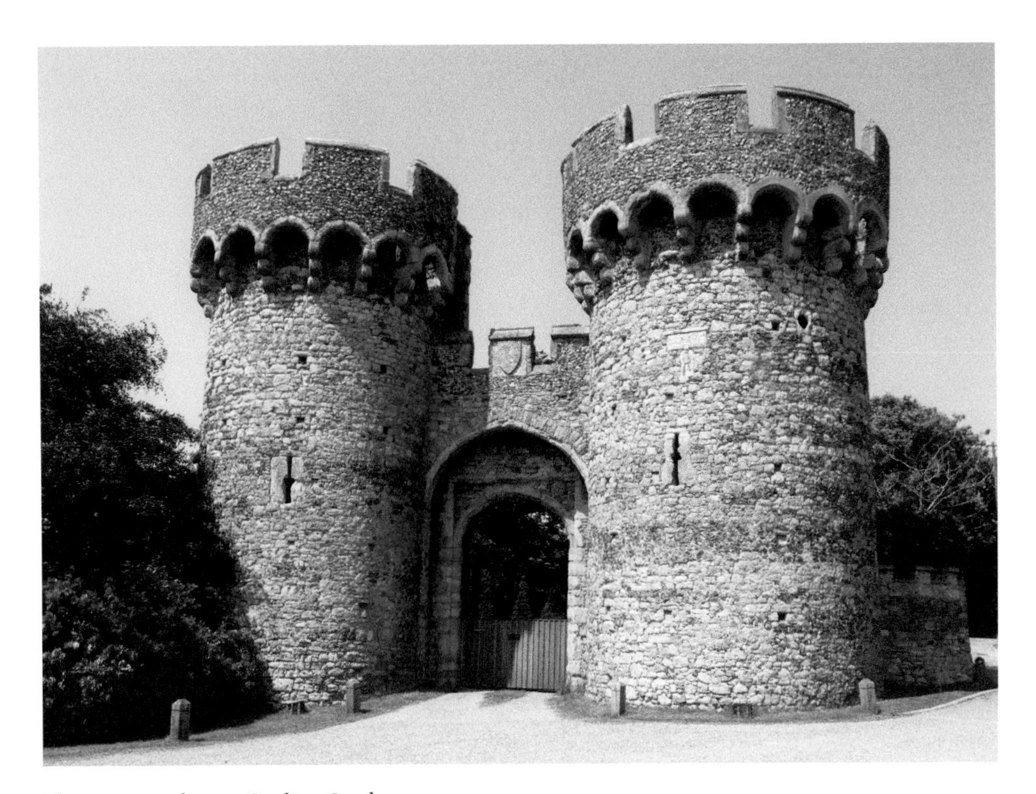

The outer gatehouse, Cooling Castle.

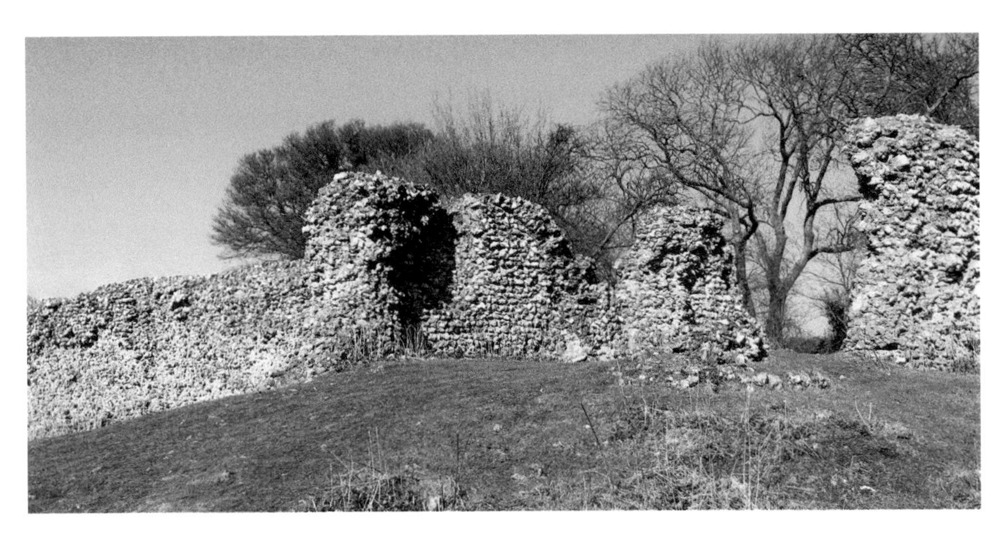

The remains of Thurnham Castle.

These new castles were square in design with a vast fortified tower (the 'keep') at the centre. Surrounding the keep were four large stone walls 10 feet–13 feet (3 metres– 4 metres) thick beyond which were ditches and banks and where possible a moat was added. A 'gatehouse' comprising a drawbridge, portcullis and large doors protected the gateway. Above the doors and behind a parapet ran a landing with openings in the floor, through which stones and boiling liquids could be dropped onto attackers. Along the walls were large towers with vertical slits allowing someone to fire arrows from inside the tower, and along the top of the wall were battlements behind which soldiers could also discharge arrows, throw boulders and pour burning liquids. The castles were designed to withstand attack from siege engines and stone-throwing weapons of the day, to provide a defensible base to garrison soldiers, and to govern the surrounding district.

One of the most striking castles built was Rochester, where today, standing defiantly amidst the ruined fortifications, can be seen one of the best-preserved Norman towers in England or France. Built to protect the River Medway, the castle was besieged three times – in 1088, 1215 and 1262 – following political disputes between Norman nobility and royalty. Built in 1127, the keep stands 100 feet (30 metres) high with walls 12 feet (4 metres) deep and is the tallest keep in England. Unlike the Saxons, the Normans recognised the importance of defending their shoreline and established castles at Dover, Saltwood and Folkestone. Although the two castles at Folkestone have disappeared, at Saltwood the gatehouse is a private residence and its walls remain almost intact, despite being deemed uninhabitable following an earthquake in 1580.

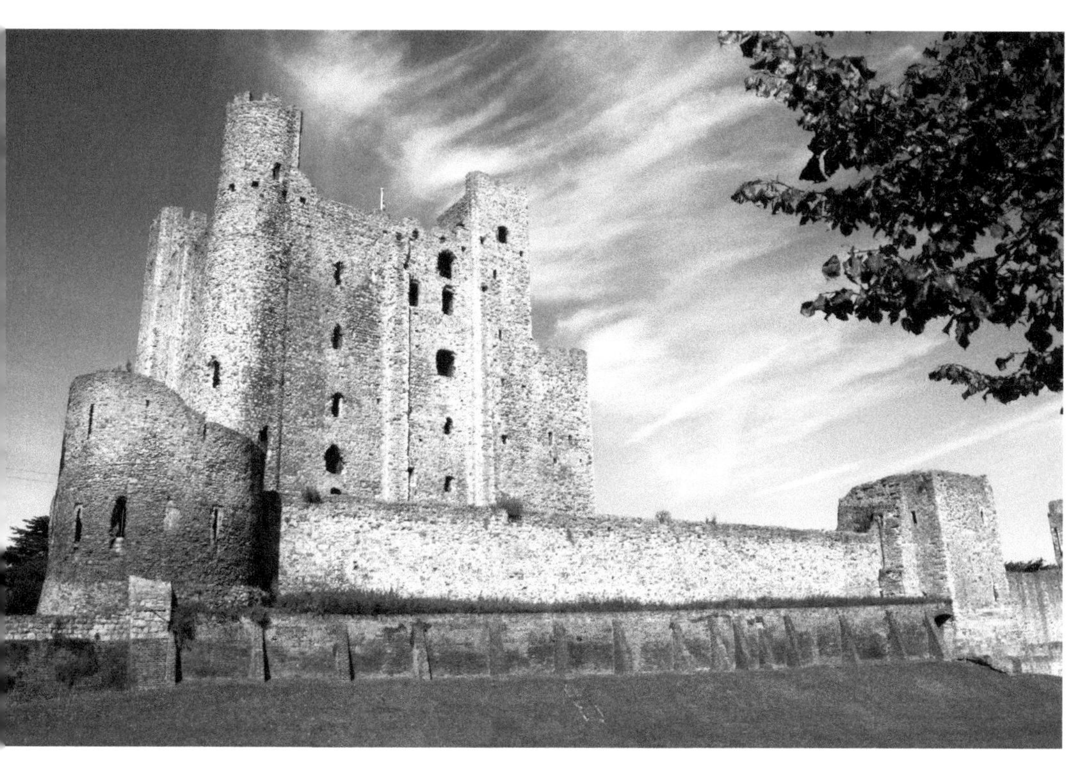

The Norman keep, Rochester Castle.

At Dover, in 1180, King Henry II built a castle upon an existing Saxon fortification which, following further improvements by his son Richard, and then John, became the first concentric castle (a castle with two or more walls, the inner walls being higher than the outer) to be built in Western Europe. Responding to sieges, attacks and threats of invasion, successive kings continued fortifying the castle adding new walls, towers and tunnels.

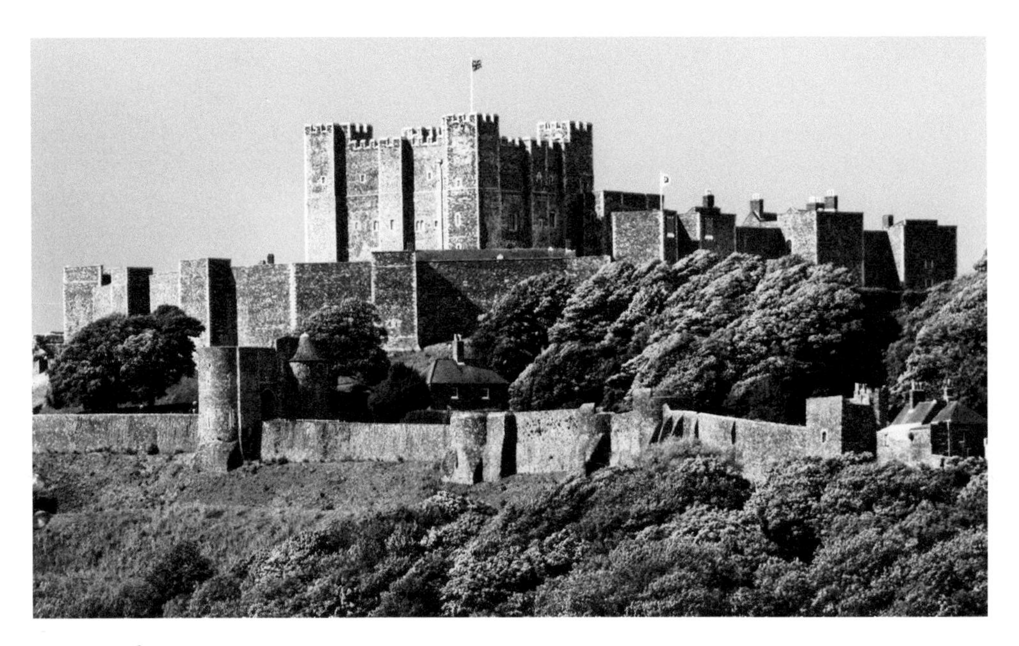

Dover Castle.

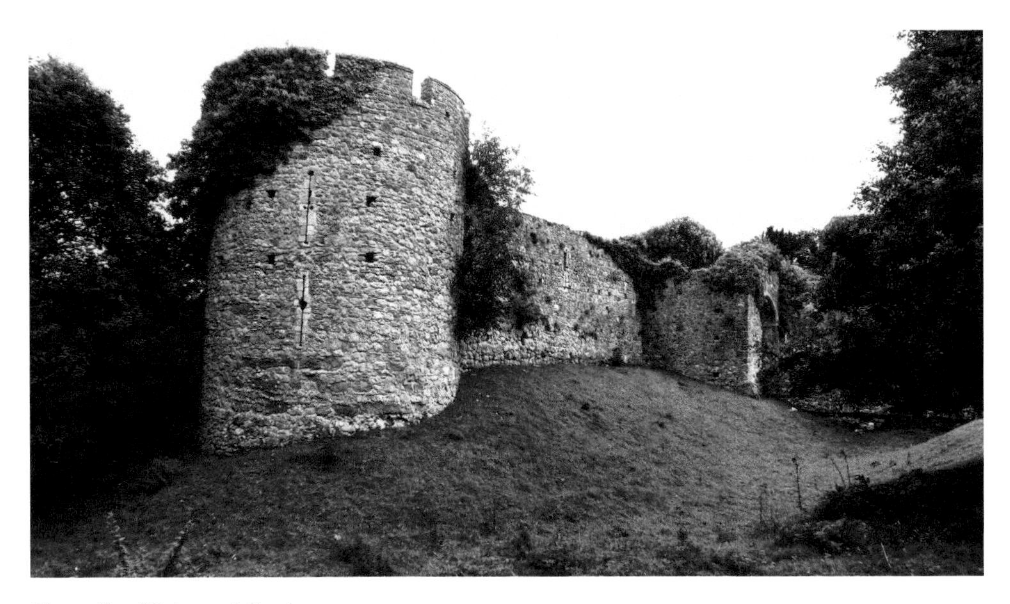

The walls of Saltwood Castle.

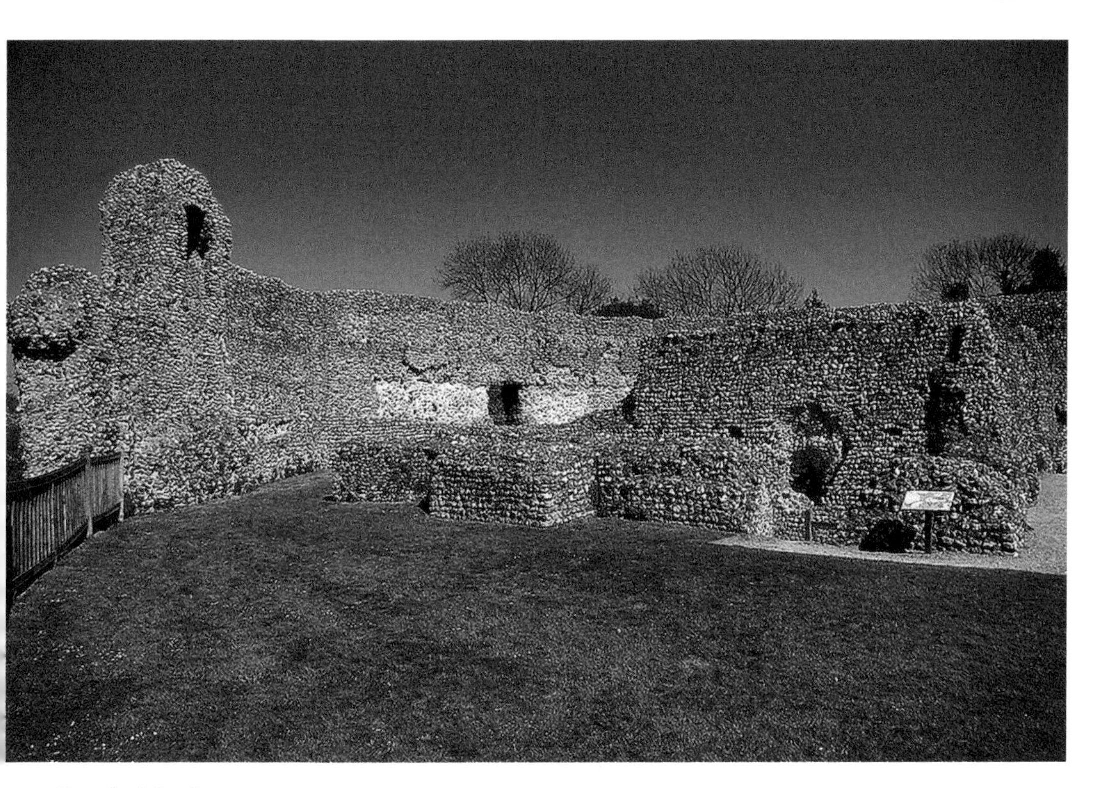

Eynsford Castle.

In contrast to most Norman castles, Eynsford was not built on the site of a motte-and-bailey castle, although a Saxon fort once sat there on an artificial mound. Built in the late eleventh century, it did not have a stone motte like most castles, rather, Eynsford was protected by an extensive curtain wall, much of which survives today at its original height, along with the remains of the hall. The first owner of Eynsford Castle, William de Eynsford I, knight and sheriff of Kent, refortified it several times, but it fell into disrepair and by the mid-eighteenth century it had become a stable and kennels for hunting hounds.

Whether intact or in ruins, Kent has many castles, all of which have played a unique part in creating the county's military heritage. For example, the once imposing Canterbury Castle was captured in 1216 by Prince Louis VIII of France, and in 1380 the army of Wat Tyler, leader of the Peasants' Revolt, stormed it. During a rebellion against Queen Mary in 1554, Sir Thomas Wyatt, en route to London, lay siege to Cooling Castle. The remains of other castles of the period, steeped in military history, can also be seen at St Leonard's, Sutton Valence and Thurnham.

Castles were used as seats of political and military authority. However, the advent of gunpowder increased an enemy's ability to cause death and destruction on a larger scale and at greater distances. As traditional defences became less effective, this innovation led to vulnerabilities that would give rise to a host of new and advanced forms of defence.

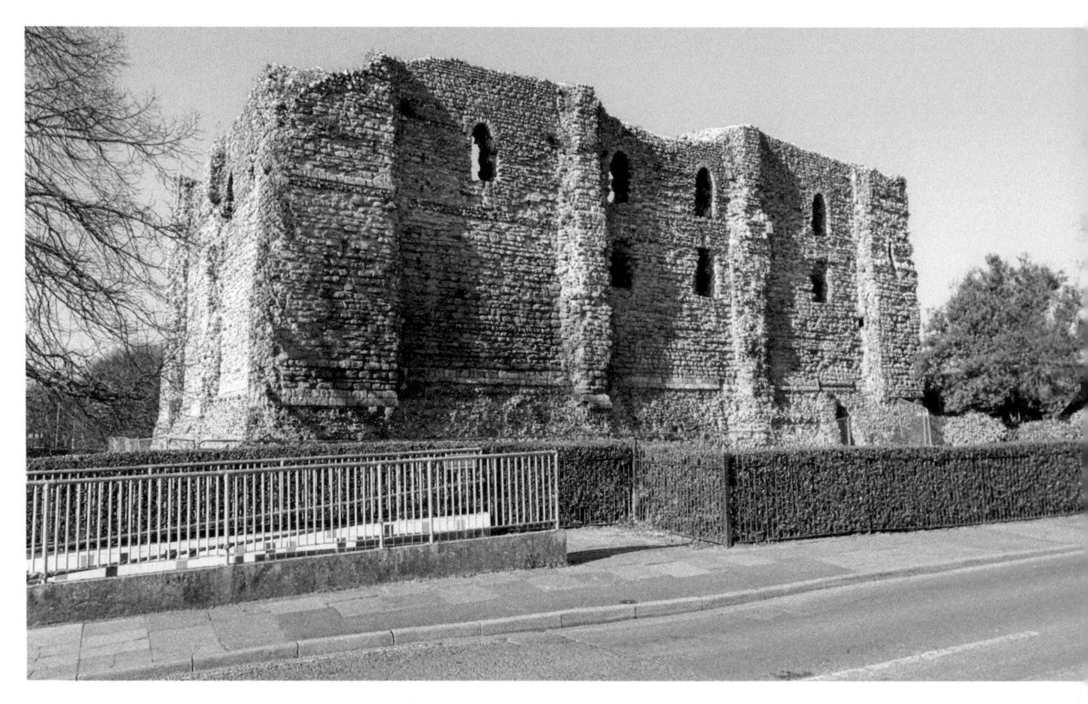

Canterbury Castle.

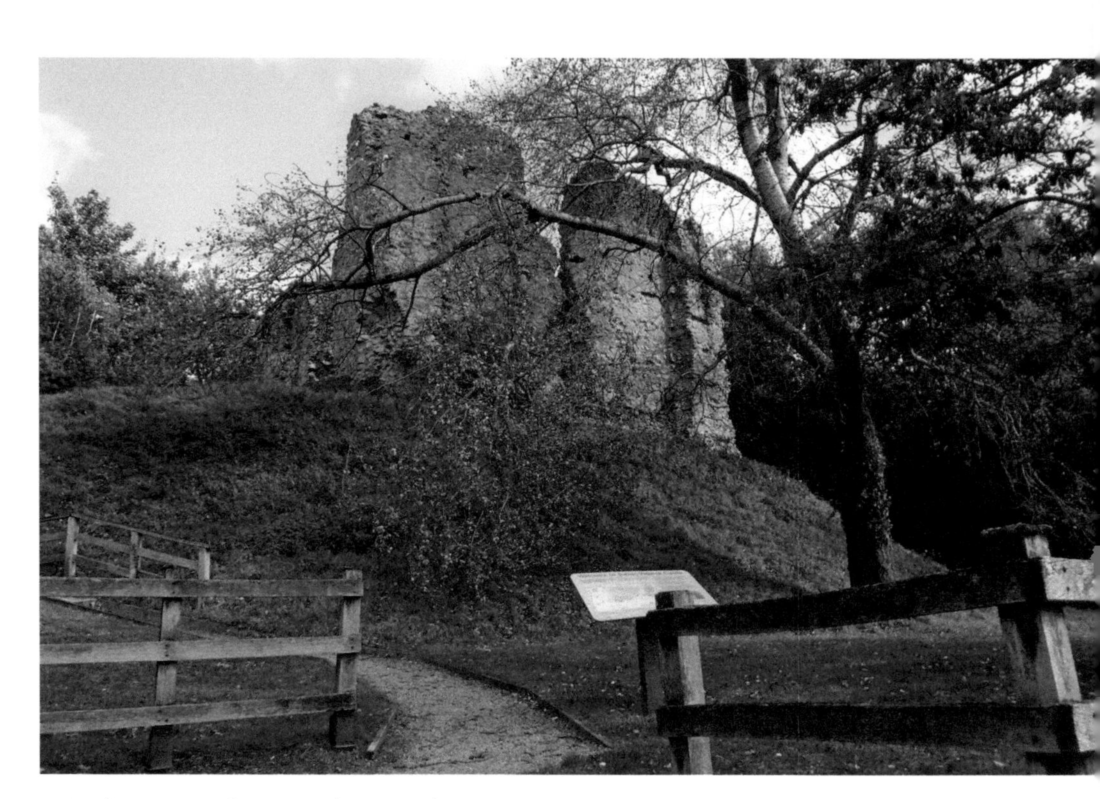

The remains of Sutton Valence Castle.

3. New Threats, New Developments

In 1345 during the Hundred Years' War, gunpowder artillery (cannons) was used for the first time on a European battlefield. Its devastating use by both sides, together with increased French attacks on shipping and coastal towns Dover, Sandwich and Folkestone, sparked fresh fears of an invasion. In response, the Crown repaired and adapted structures under its control, while townships and barons improved their fortifications. In towns such as Rochester, Dover and Canterbury, defensive walls and turrets were modified, new cannon positions added and arrow loops (narrow vertical openings originally designed for archers) were modified by adding a large circle at the bottom, creating 'keyhole'-style gun ports that allowed modern firearms to be used.

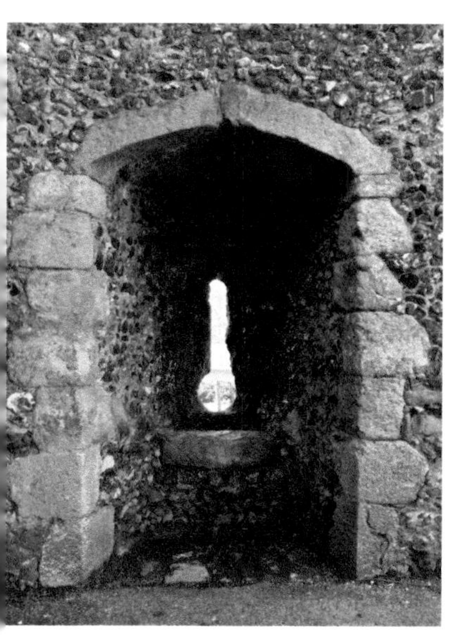

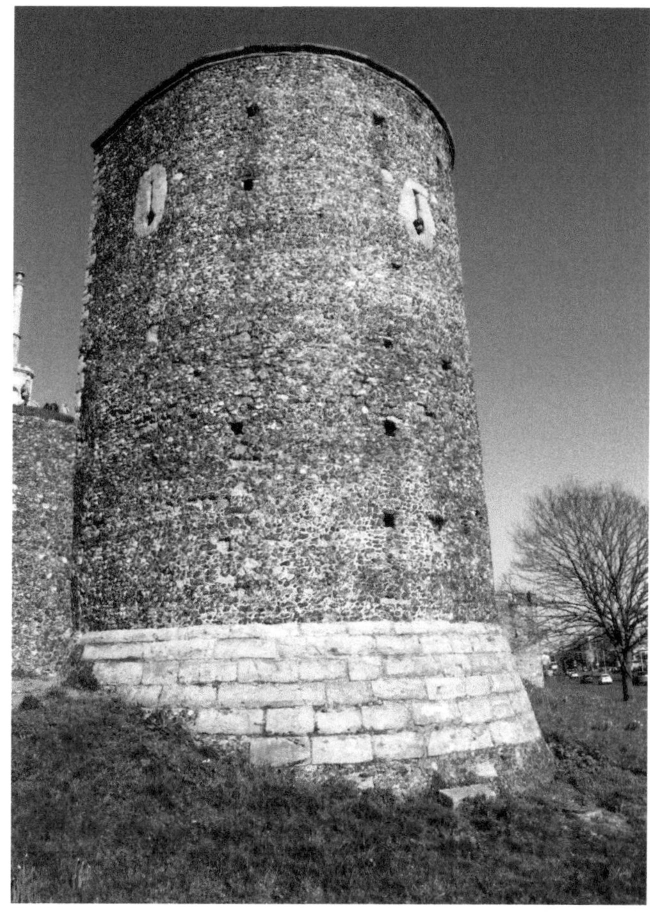

Above: Gun port, from inside turret, Canterbury city walls.

Right: Keyhole gun port, Canterbury city walls.

Just as the Roman catapults and ballista proved too much for Celtic hill forts, Norman castles were no longer impregnable strongholds. Developments in firearms and cannons continued to impact the evolution of defensive systems and warfare. By the sixteenth century, range, accuracy, destructive power, new ordnance, solid/scatter shot, incendiary devices, and exploding shells saw defensive structures dramatically change in style, design and functionality. Forts became less visible, less vulnerable and more capable of stopping invaders out at sea before they could land troops.

Besides expanding his navy, King Henry VIII issued an order called a 'Device' to build new-style artillery fortifications at key coastal locations and naval dockyards. Known as 'Device Forts' or Henrician castles, they were resistant to the effects of enemy cannons, providing long-range defensive fire. In Kent, castles were built at Deal, Walmer and Sandwich. Although each castle varied, their design was principally the same. Built into the ground, they were circular with thick, round stone walls that deflected rather than absorbed incoming cannon shot. Unlike the towering walls and keeps of Norman castles, each presented a low profile to attackers with a short bastion at its centre. The bastion housed bespoke cannon positions built into the thick fort walls, surrounded by up to six low platforms capped with large cannons. Although an improvement against attackers at a distance, the cannons couldn't fire upon ground in front of their position. The resultant 'dead ground' made the castle vulnerable to attack from close quarters.

The invasion fears of Henry VIII's reign passed, resulting in some Device Forts in Kent being completely demolished. Sandown Fort, near Deal, was partially demolished in 1882, its remains now forming part of the seawall. The remnants of Sandgate, Henry's first

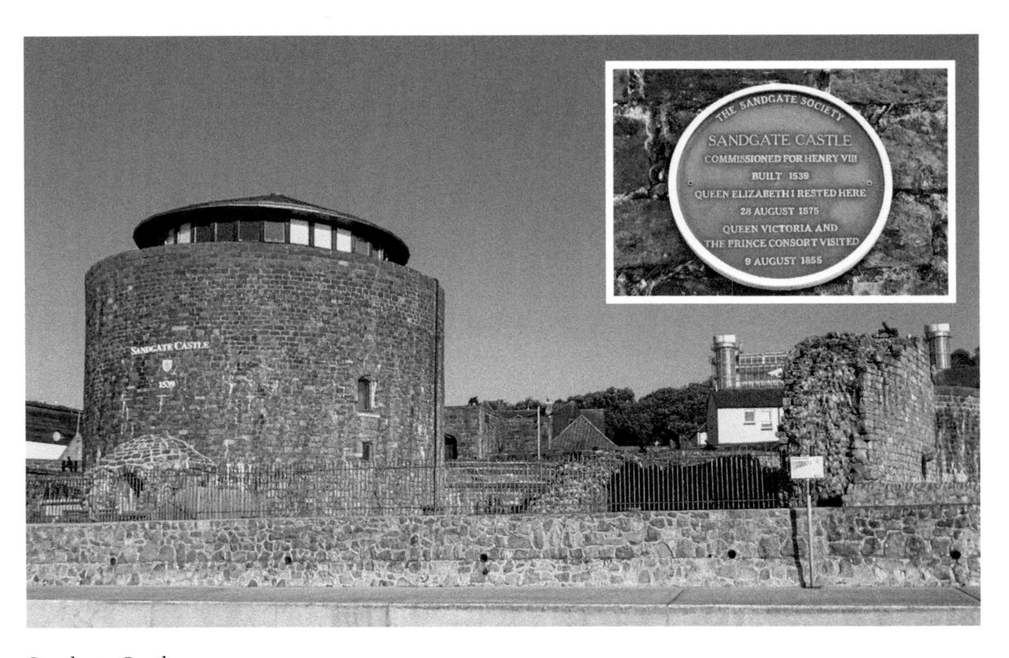

Sandgate Castle.

Inset: Blue plaque.

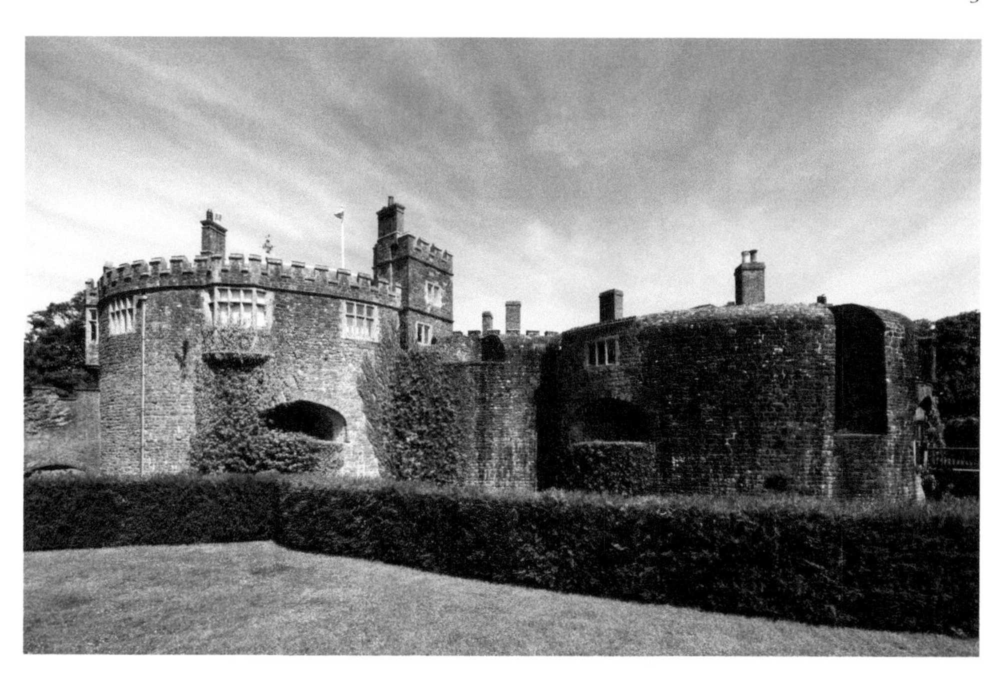

Walmer Castle.

Device Fort, are more formidable, but by far the best examples are at Walmer and Deal, where both remain intact. Deal was the largest of the Device fortifications with six inner and outer bastions, housing sixty-six artillery firing positions.

The Great Turf, the Little Turf, the Great White and the Black Bulwarks were part of the Device fortifications but are now destroyed. They were known as 'Bulwarks' and formed a defensive chain of earthworks linked by trenches that run between Sandown and Walmer.

To engage enemy shipping and protect the Thames Estuary, Henry built five new-style fortifications called 'blockhouses'. These were two storeys high and built of brick, following the concentric design: low thick walls, fronted by a D-shaped bastion and rounded parapet designed to deflect cannon shot. A stone tower stood in the centre, with internal gun ports and a rooftop gun platform. Cannons fired from behind large earthen ramparts on either side of the fort provided added protection from enemy guns. Two blockhouses were built in Kent. At Gravesend the foundations of the Milton Blockhouse remain at the western end of the canal basin, while the foundations of another lie under the lawn and car park in front of the Clarendon Royal Hotel. Although innovative, their design meant they could not offer defensive crossfire, creating vulnerable 'dead areas' from which they could be attacked.

The next development in fortifications saw the introduction of pointed angular bastions to solve the problem of 'dead ground'. Two such buildings were constructed in Kent, one at the rear of the Milton Blockhouse, which is now gone but its location is 'surface marked' for visitors. The other was built in front of Upnor Castle on the River Medway, protecting passage to the Royal Dockyard at Chatham and military locations at Rochester and Gillingham. In addition, the installation of additional blockhouses and bulwarks improved the Medway's defences.

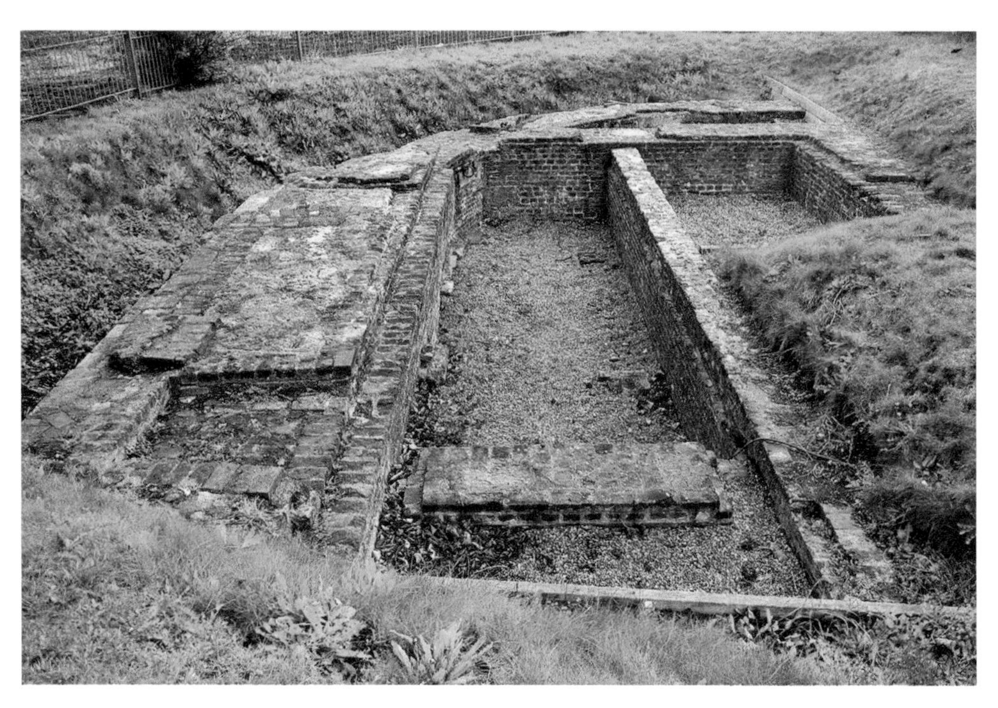

Remains of Milton Blockhouse.

In 1667, Upnor Castle and the blockhouses failed to stop the Dutch navy en route to the Royal Dockyard at Chatham and further fortifications were needed. The largest scheme of artillery defence ever seen was undertaken at Sheerness at the mouth of the Medway, where the nation's second Royal Dockyard was being established. Further inland along the banks of the river, new gun batteries were built at Cockham Wood and Gillingham.

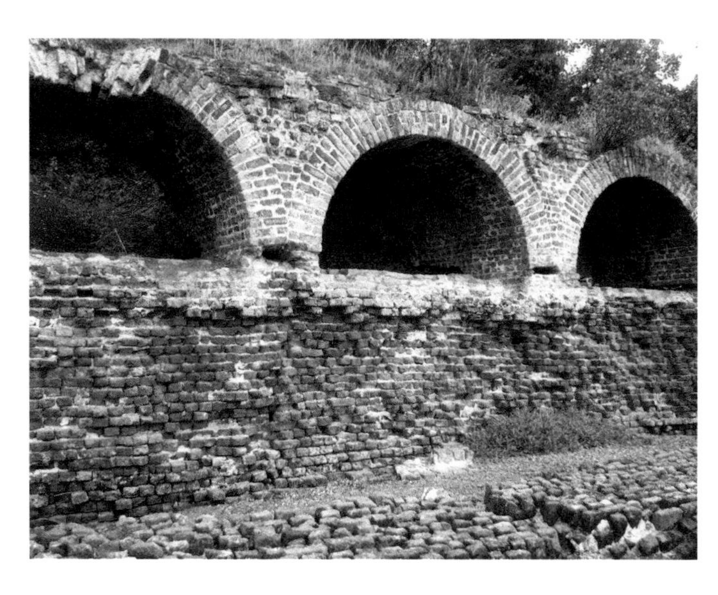

Remains of Cockham Woods Fort.

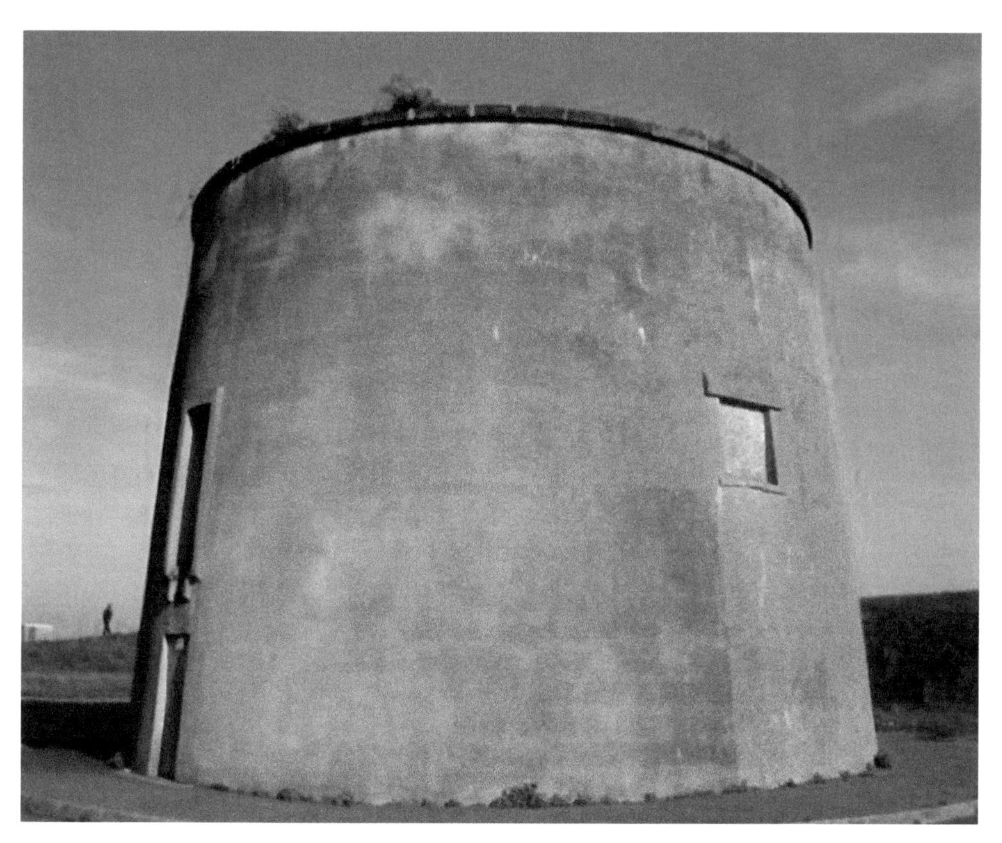

Dymchurch Martello Tower No. 24. (SP.)

During the French Revolutionary War (1792–1802) and the Napoleonic Wars (1803–1815), the French continued to fuel speculation that Napoleon's invasion of Britain, unprecedented in scale, was imminent. Countermeasures had to be proportionate and a defensive line of circular fortified buildings was built along the south and east coasts. Based on a tower whose defensibility had impressed the British naval forces at Mortella Point, Corsica, they called them 'Martello Towers'. They stood at 40 feet (12 metres) with walls 8 feet (2.4 metres) thick, and were constructed around a central brick pillar. Equipped with a roof cannon, they housed a garrison of one officer and fifteen to twenty-five men. Between 1805 and 1812, 103 towers were built, with numbers 1–74 stretching from Folkestone to Seaford, Sussex. Of the forty-five remaining, many exist as ruins, but the best preserved is No. 24 at Dymchurch. Now restored, it serves as a museum of life in the tower.

The Royal Military Canal was built to stall an invading force until reinforcements could arrive, protecting the Romney Marsh coast. It was cut between 1805–09. At 30 feet (10 metres) wide and running for 26 miles (42 km), it is Britain's third-longest defensive monument after Hadrian's Wall and Offa's Dyke. Designed as a series of 1,500-foot (457-metre) staggered stretches, each return housed an artillery battery capable of firing its gun the length of the next stretch.

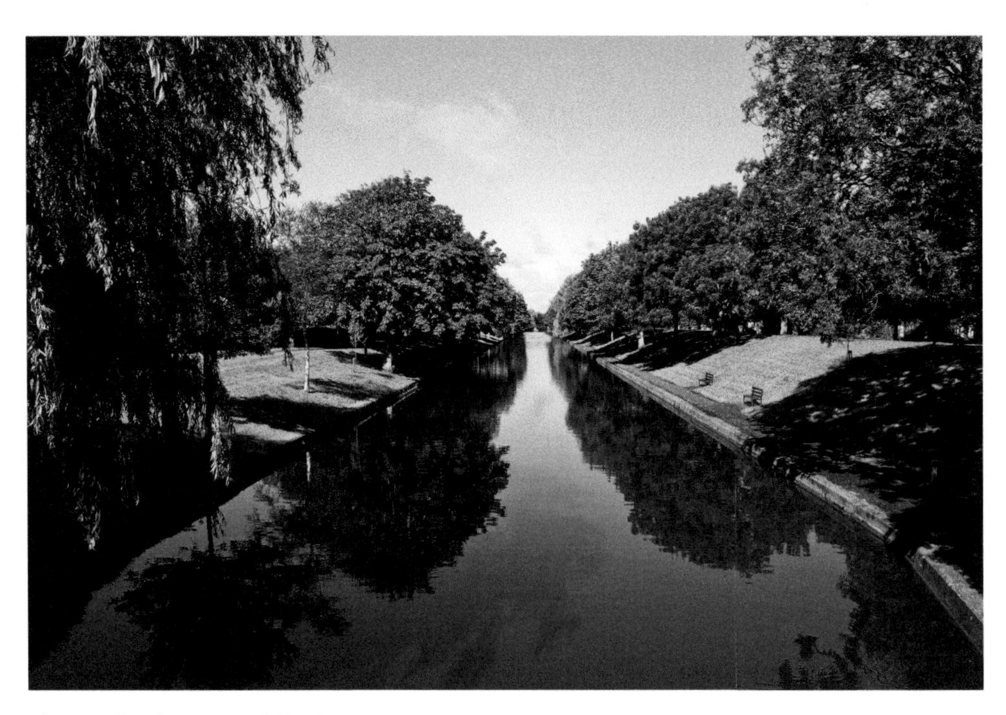

The Royal Military Canal. (DT.)

Gun batteries made of shingle were built at Dungeness to protect the vulnerable peninsular and secured within brick retaining walls. Arranged in an arc protecting offshore anchorage, they were equipped with new traversing platforms that utilised metal rails to manoeuvre guns into position. Of these four batteries, the remains of No. 1's gun emplacement exist at Lydd-on-Sea. At Lade, No. 2 was used as a coastguard station during the nineteenth century, and then an anti-aircraft gun site during both World Wars. Today only the gun emplacement remains. Between 1818–23, the sea destroyed No. 3 and No. 4 batteries.

By the mid-nineteenth century Britain had made an uneasy alliance with France, whose fleet of ironclad ships was threatening the Royal Navy's long-held supremacy of the sea. Despite decades of peace, another revolution and a failed coup in 1848, fears of a French invasion never ceased. Forts using bastions, with flanking batteries and carefully constructed lines of fire, were now vulnerable to the effects of new entrenching tactics, exploding shells and rifled artillery. The response saw new polygonal-style fortifications being built. Polygonal forts were defensive bunkers formed with straight-lined ramparts, behind which low-level bomb-proof corridors were located, providing a protective means of access to the outworks. In addition, defenders could fire from safety along the ditches. Shornemead at Gravesend, Kent's only polygonal fort, was built to guard the entrance to the Thames.

When tensions between France, Italy and Austria led to the Second Italian War of Independence in 1859, concerns about the strength and activities of the French Navy rekindled fears of another European war and invasion of Britain. In 1860, the Royal

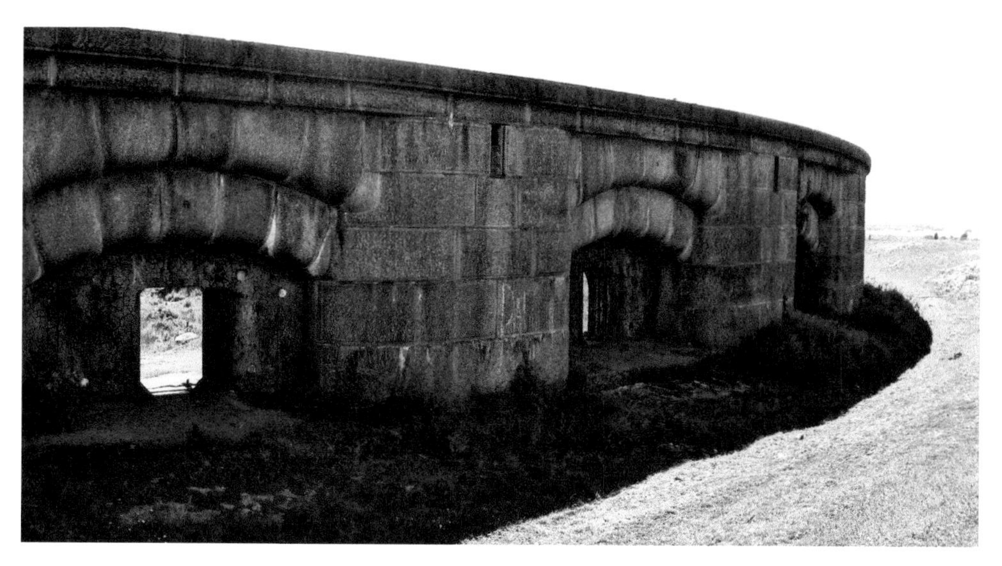

Shornemead Fort.

Commission on the Defence of the United Kingdom directed a new programme of defensive works. Championed by Lord Palmerston, the then prime minister, the forts became known as 'Palmerston Forts'. Defending the Naval Dockyard at Chatham from seaborne attack, twenty such forts were built along the rivers Thames and Medway. Well-fortified, they varied in design, with many being adapted for use during the Second World War. Outstanding examples of those remaining include Forts Hoo, Darnet, Garrison Point, Luton, New Tavern and Slough, along with Castle Hill Fort at Dover.

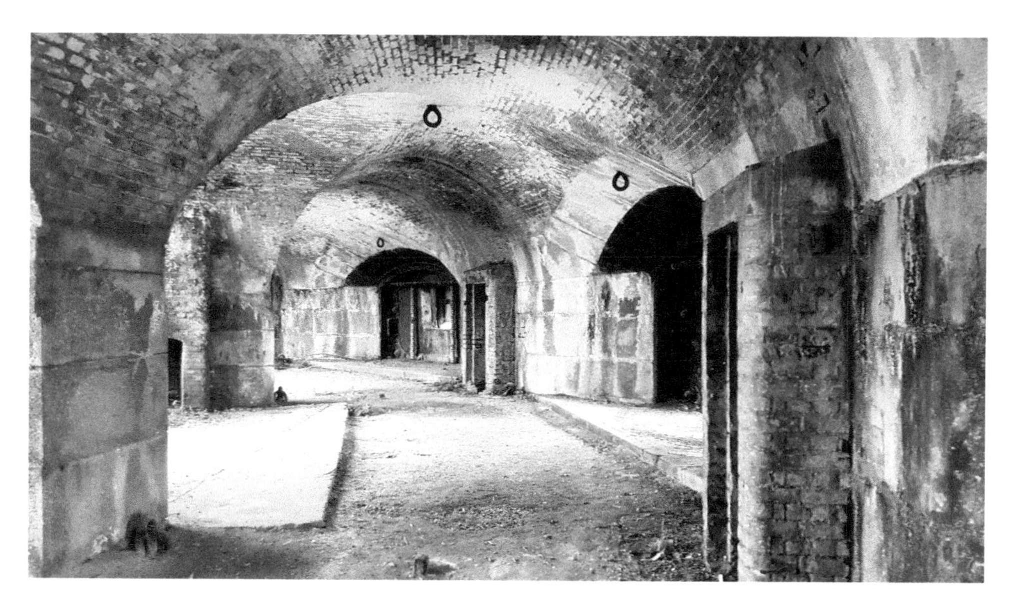

Fort Hoo.

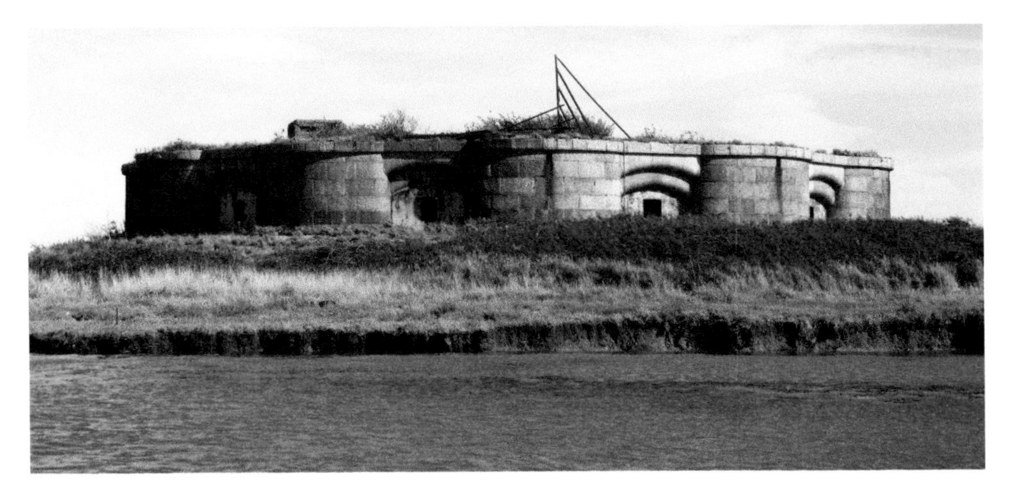

Fort Darnet.

With continued technological advances in the field of weaponry, the process of improving and adapting Kent's coastal defences became an ongoing programme. At the turn of the century, breech-loading guns replaced cannons, and pillboxes were sited at vulnerable locations such as harbours, beachfronts and open countryside. The First World War saw new weapons, submarines and aeroplanes threatening Britain's shores for the first time and once again public fear of invasion was aroused.

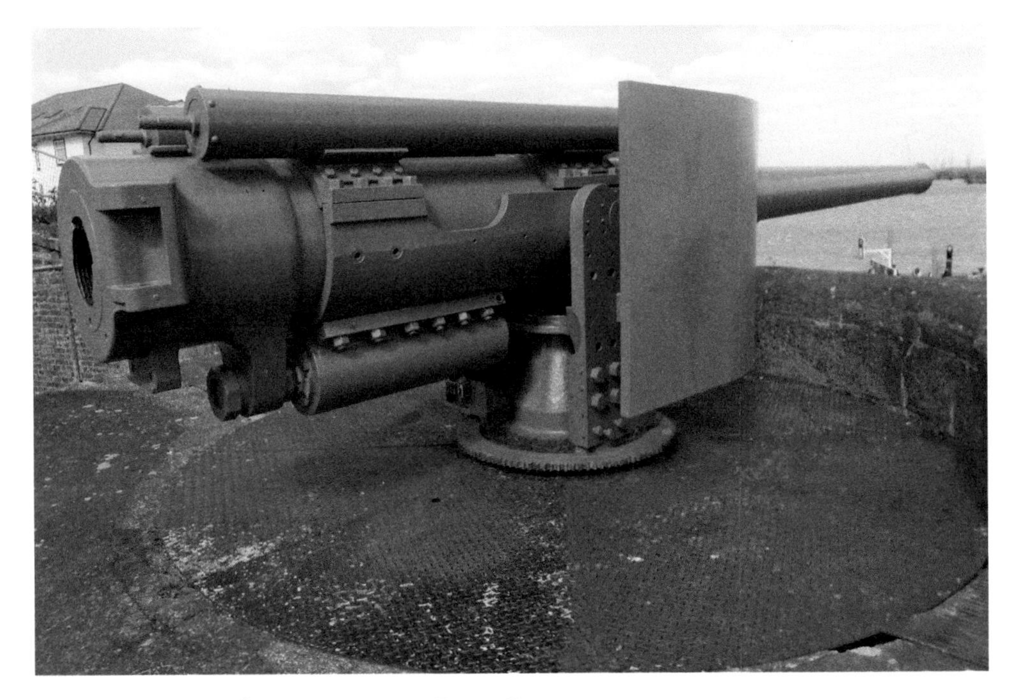

Breech-loading coastal gun 1904–08, New Tavern Fort.

In addition, new brick-built machine-gun emplacements and large searchlights were installed at artillery batteries, forts, docks, airfields and barracks. Protecting the Isles of Grain and Sheppey along with the North Downs, a series of defensive 'stop lines' (anti-invasion measures) were installed. These included concrete pillboxes, barbed-wire entanglements, artillery positions and anti-aircraft guns, and became known as the Chatham Land Front. Vast minefields were created to defend the coastal waters and plans laid for hanging anti-submarine nets across the Straits of Dover, although this idea never materialised. Along the rivers Thames and Medway, existing fortifications were upgraded with new powerful breech-loading guns. Airfields were built at Bekesbourne, Detling and Throwley and in response to the first Zeppelin airship raids, experimental sound detection systems were deployed. These employed a mixture of large mobile trumpets and massive fixed concave concrete acoustic mirrors; today the remains of two of these mirrors can be seen at Fan Bay, Dover. Later versions from the 1920s are viewable at Dungeness.

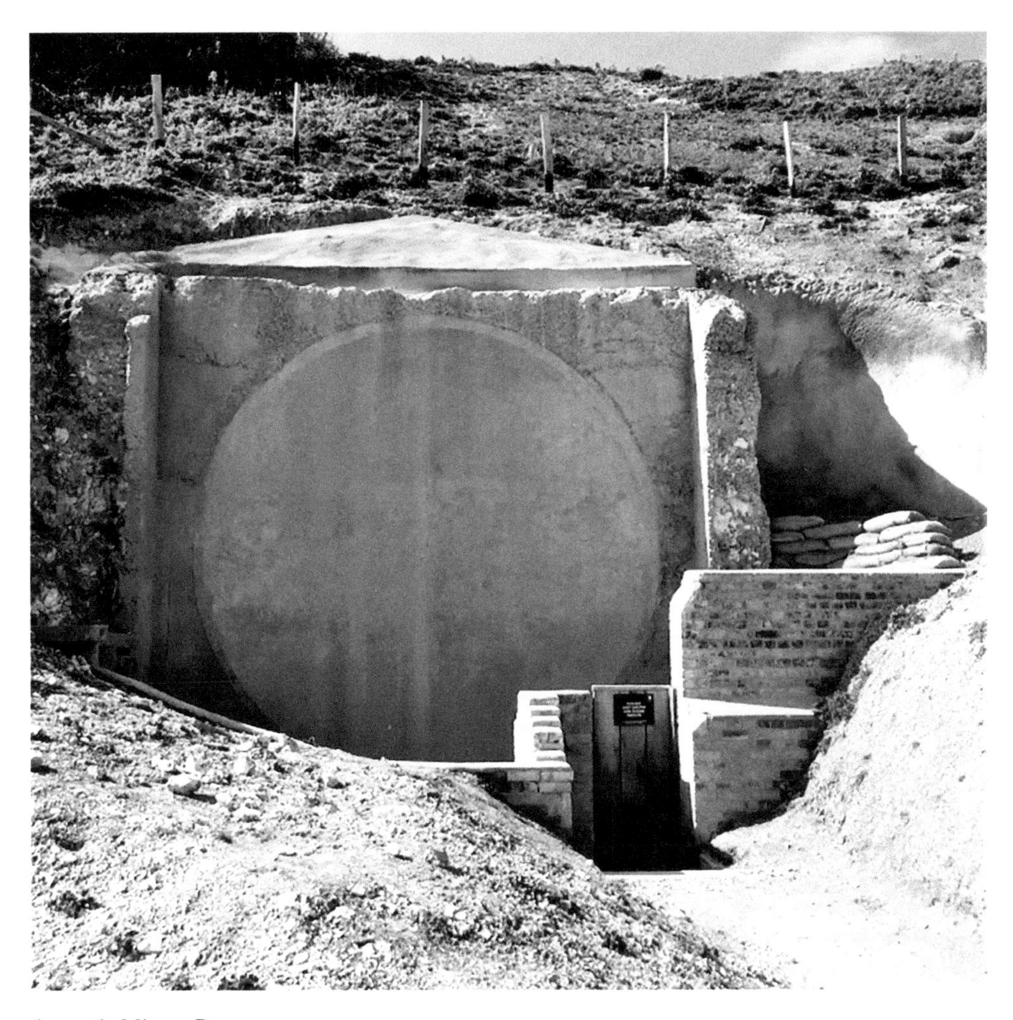

Acoustic Mirror, Dover.

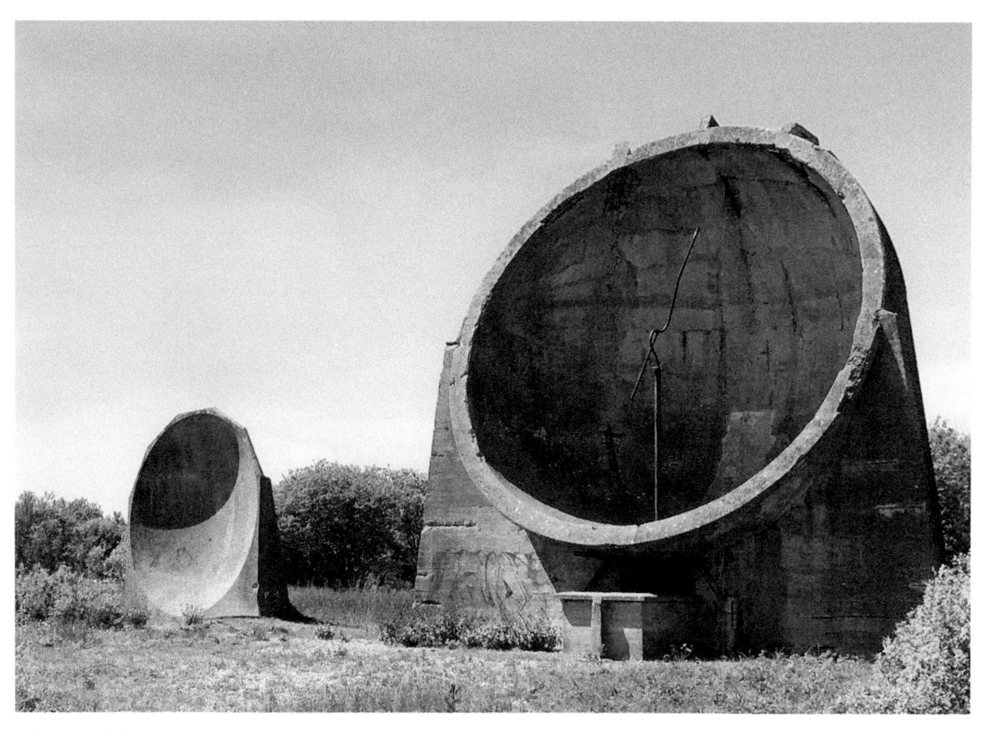

Above and below: Acoustic Mirror, Denge.

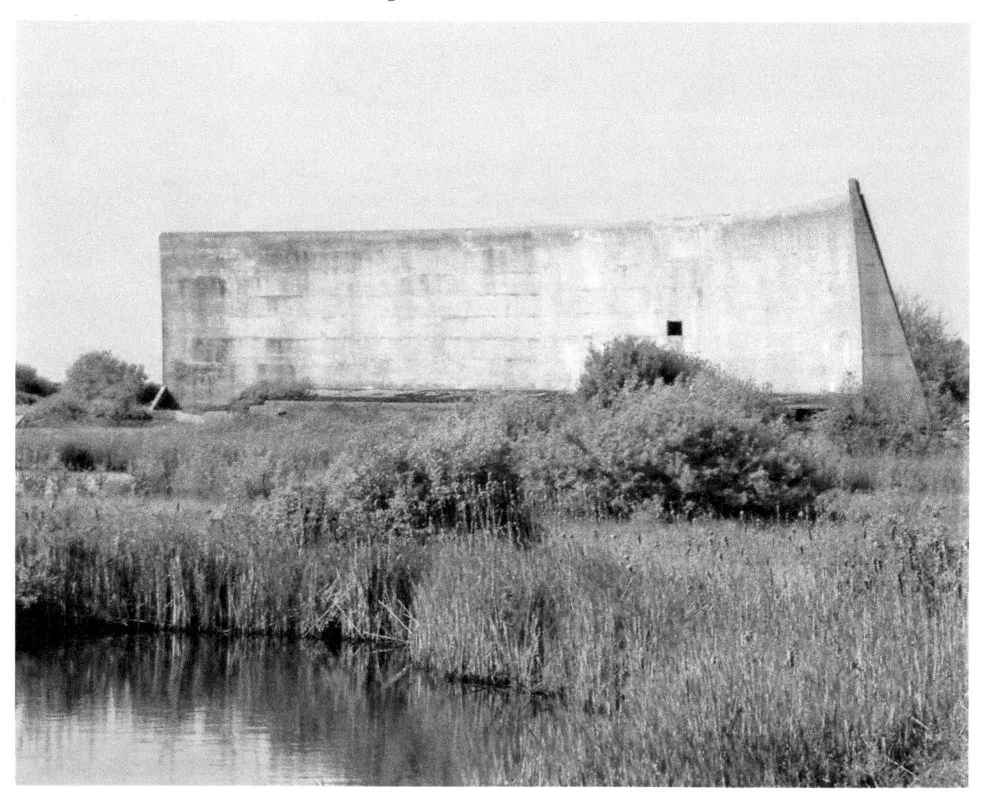

During the Second World War, Britain would again 'gird its loins' against attack as the coast once more became the nation's front line against invasion. In May 1940, Commander-in-Chief Home Forces General Sir Edmund Ironside ordered the fortification of potential landing beaches and areas inland, creating what he termed the 'coastal crust'. Not designed to stop German forces landing, the coastal crust merely created a delay until reinforcements inland could mount a counter-attack. Using fixed defences, lighter

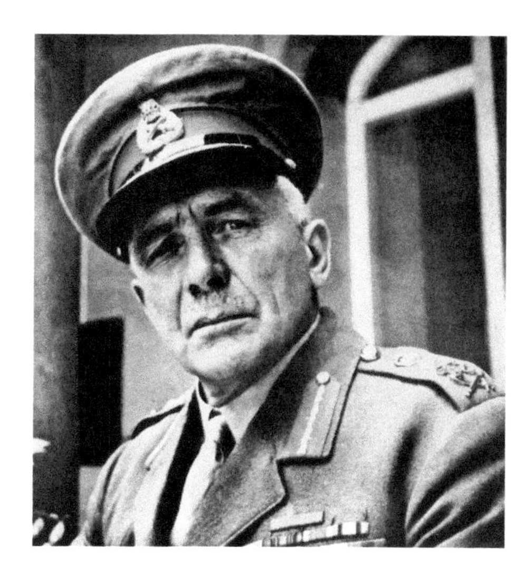

Right: General Edmund Ironside.

Below: Anti-tank defences, Isle of Grain.

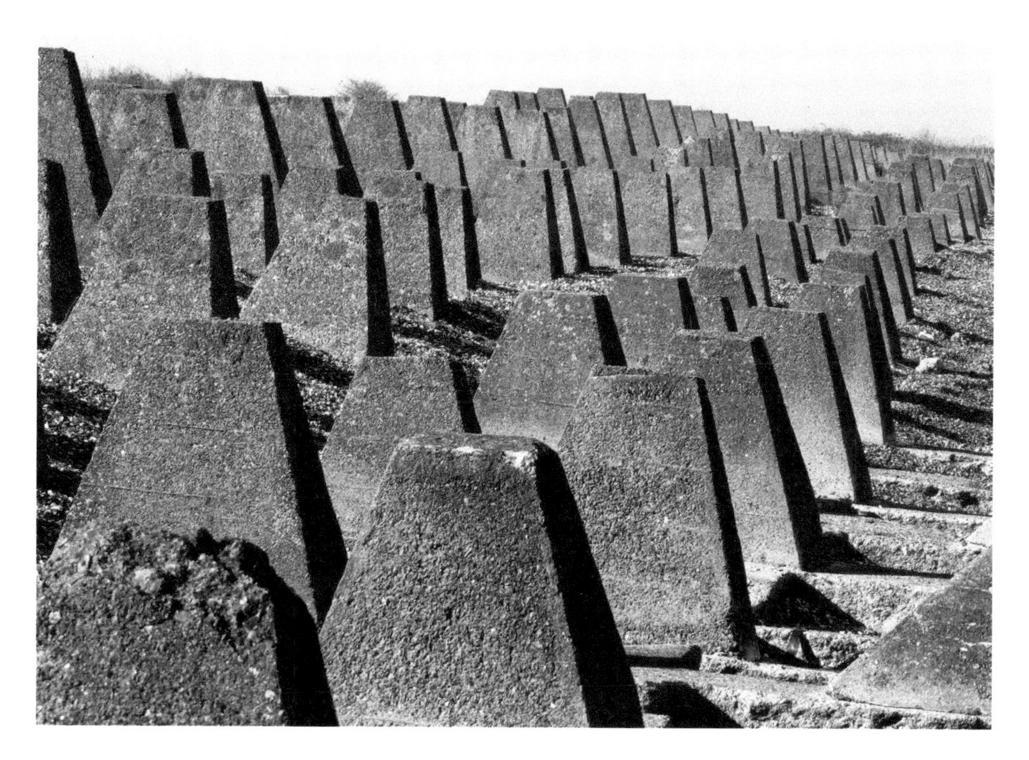

artillery, small arms and mines, coastal fortifications were responsible for hampering, delaying and breaking up an initial attack. Inland, defensive lines were constructed using anti-tank blockhouses, entrenchments, vehicle obstacles, roadblocks, pillboxes, natural barriers, mortar sites and minefields. These were intended to slow down German attempts to move inland and prevent the fast-moving armoured sweeps seen across Europe. Remnants can still be seen today throughout the county.

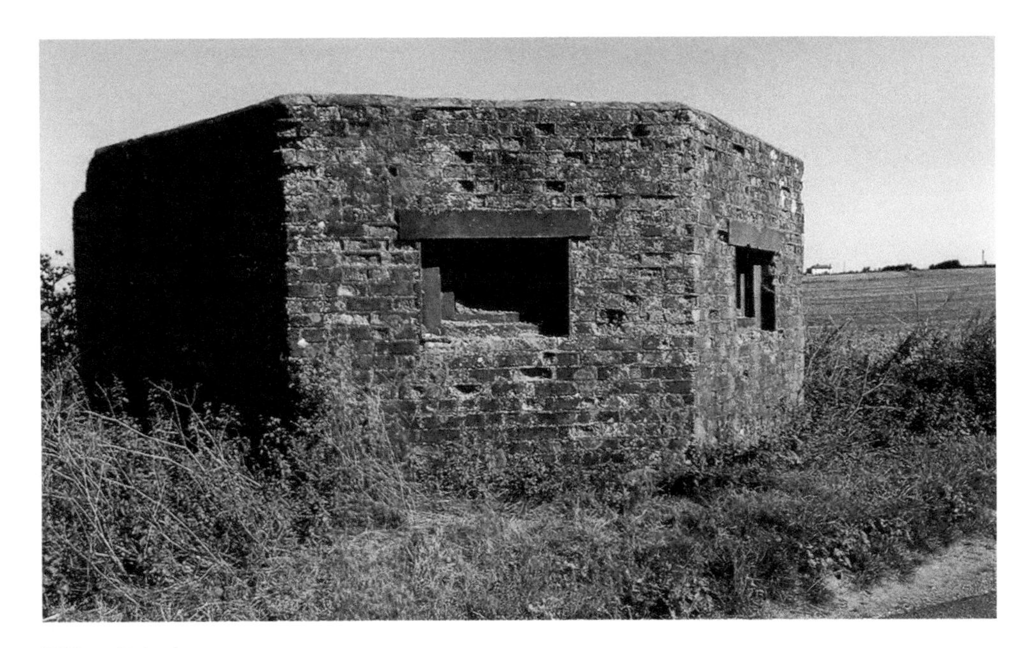

Pillbox, Bekesbourne.

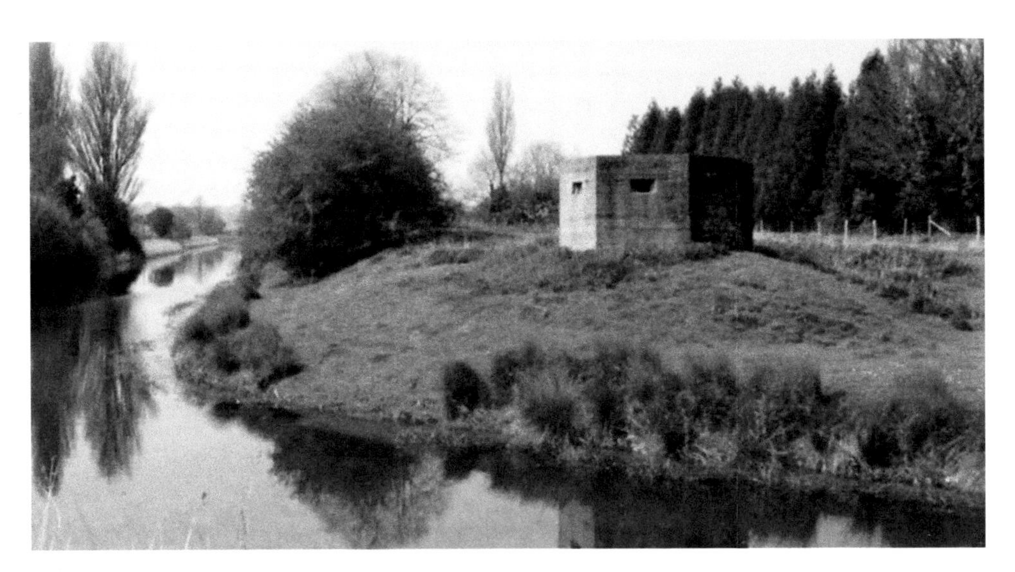

Type 22 Pillbox, Royal Military Canal. (PS, PSG).

A successful amphibious invasion would need air supremacy followed by an initial assault of paratroopers and gliders. Open spaces prickled with poles criss-crossed with wire and explosives deployed to prevent and destroy glider landings. To deter the Luftwaffe from laying mines in the waterways and using the River Thames as a navigational landmark, new 'Maunsell' forts were positioned in the Thames Estuary at Tongue and Shivering Sands. Built in two distinctive army and navy designs, they were floated to their locations and secured on the seabed. The navy design, like early offshore oil platforms, comprised a rectangular 168-foot by 88-foot (51-metre by 27-metre) reinforced concrete pontoon base, with a supporting superstructure of two 60-foot- (18-metre-) tall, 24-foot- (7.3-metre-) round hollow reinforced concrete towers. The Tongue Sands Fort was placed 6 miles (10.2 km) off the coast of Margate. The army design included seven larger interconnected steel tripod-style platforms. The Shivering Sands Fort was located 9 miles (14 km) from Herne Bay.

The greatest threat to Britain came from the air. Fighter bombers attacked ports, docks and airfields and heavy bombers targeted industrial sites and cities, while Hitler's railway

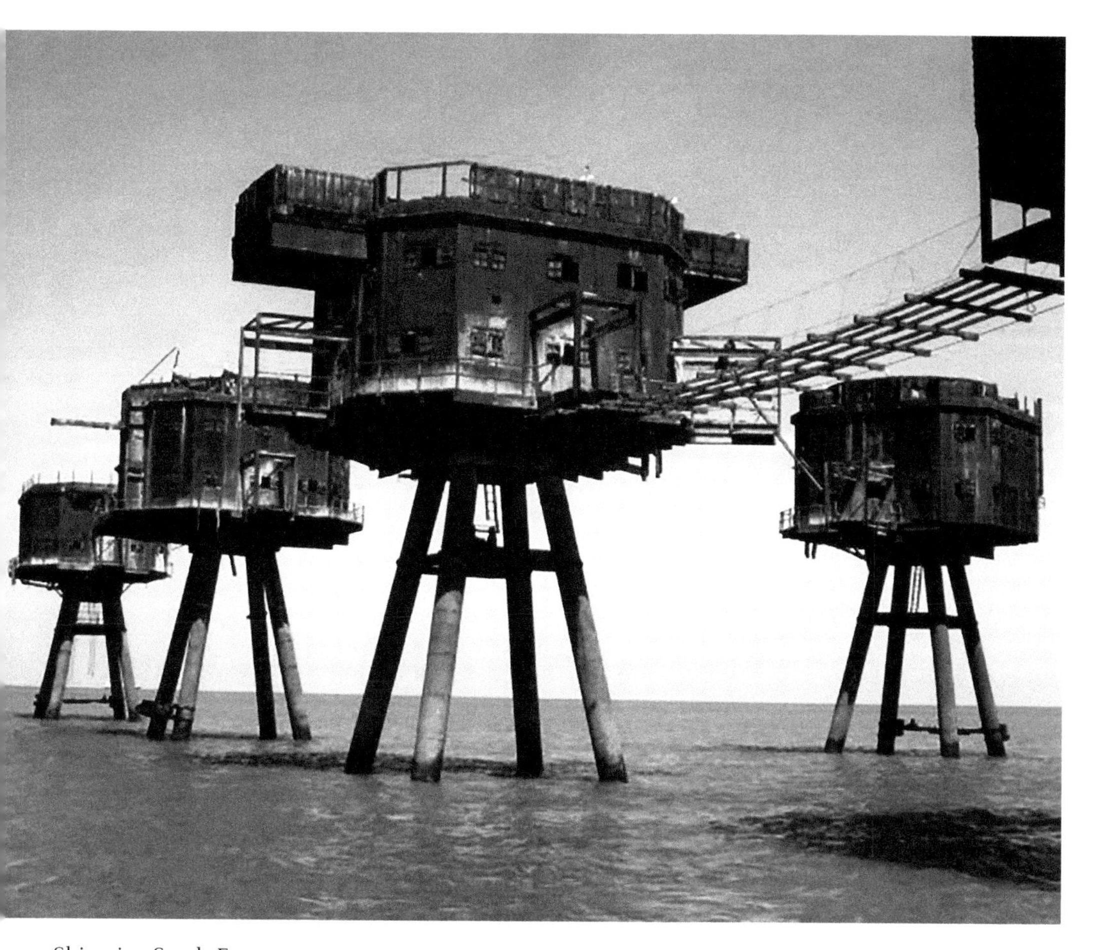

Shivering Sands Fort.

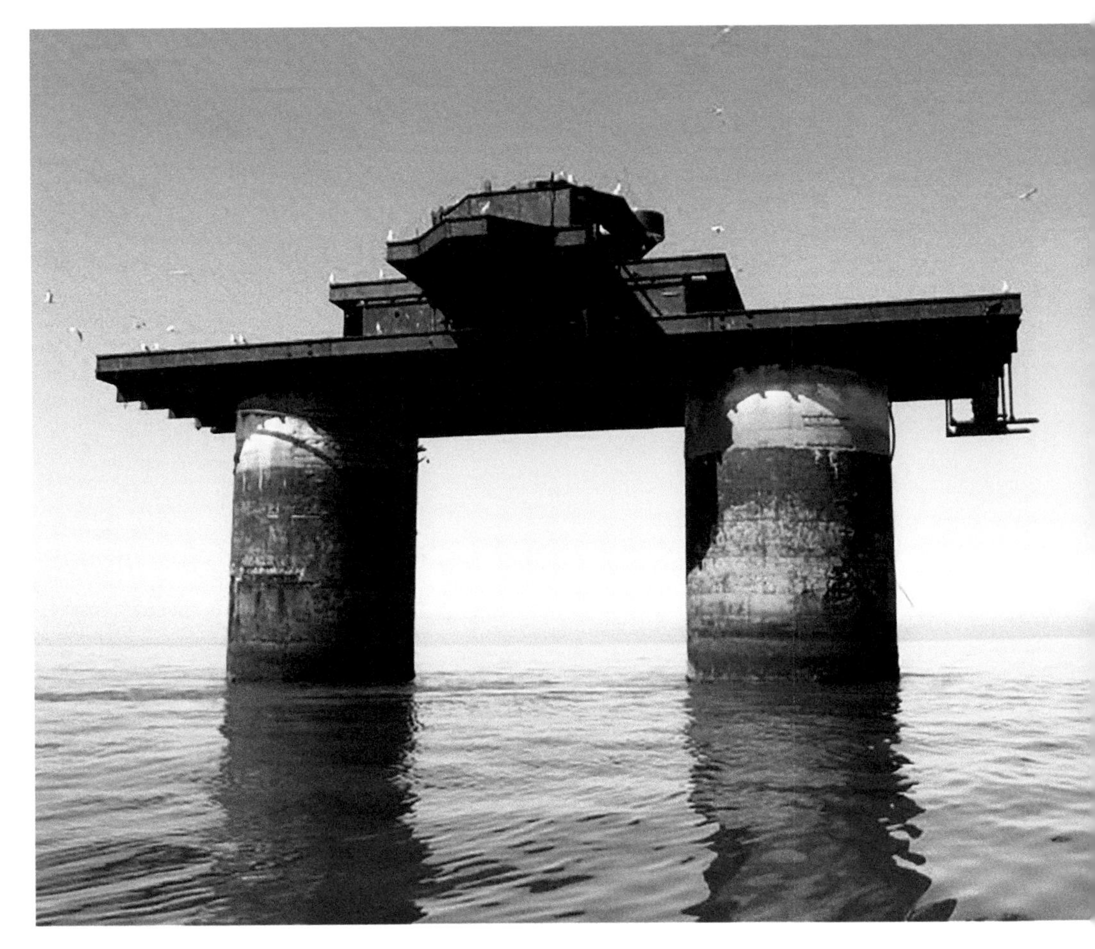

Tongue Sands Fort.

guns and vengeance weapons – the V1 flying Bomb, V2 Rocket and V3 Supergun – struck from afar. The government provided private and communal air-raid shelters to safeguard the public from bombing raids and later V1 bombs, but nothing could stop or protect against attacks from V2 Rockets. To counter the Luftwaffe, Kent used eight military airfields: Biggin Hill, Manston, Hawkinge, Gravesend, Eastchurch, Detling, Lympne and West Malling. Each played a decisive part in the county's defence.

Chain Home, 'CH', was the code name for a ring of early-warning radar stations built along the coast by the Royal Air Force (RAF). This ring served as the world's first integrated air defence system designed to detect and track incoming enemy aircraft. Radar transmitting stations located at Swingate, Dunkirk and New Church provided the RAF with thirty minutes' warning of an incoming threat.

The peace of 1945 gave way to the Cold War in 1946, creating a new threat of nuclear attack. During the 1950s and '60s, nuclear observation posts, fallout and monitoring shelters and civil defence bunkers were built across the UK to accommodate key officials and dignitaries from the government, emergency services, military and sciences.

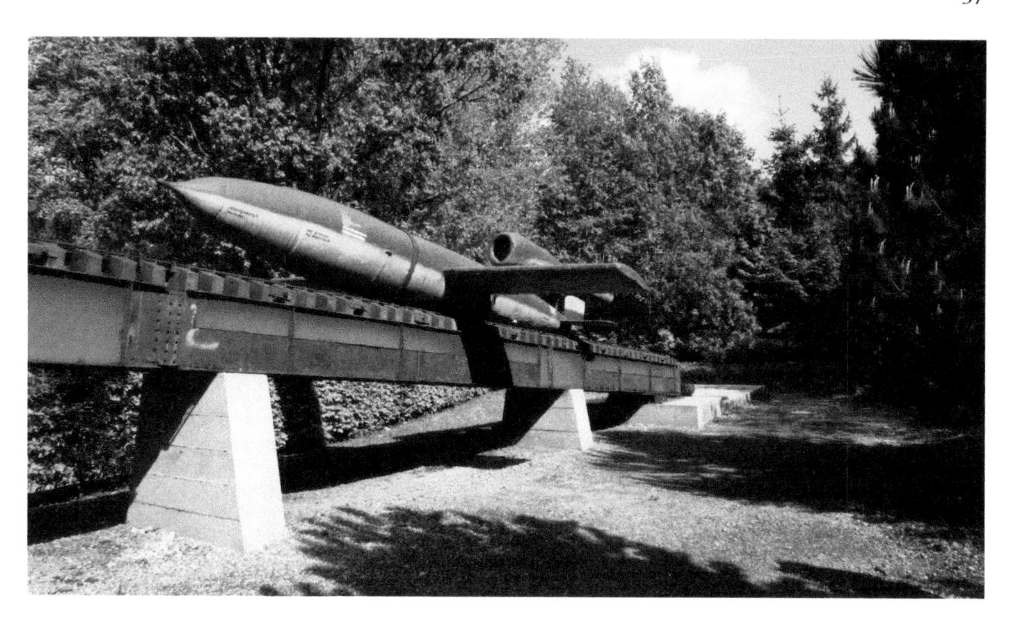

Above: V1 flying bomb. (DT.)

Right: V2 rocket. (DT.)

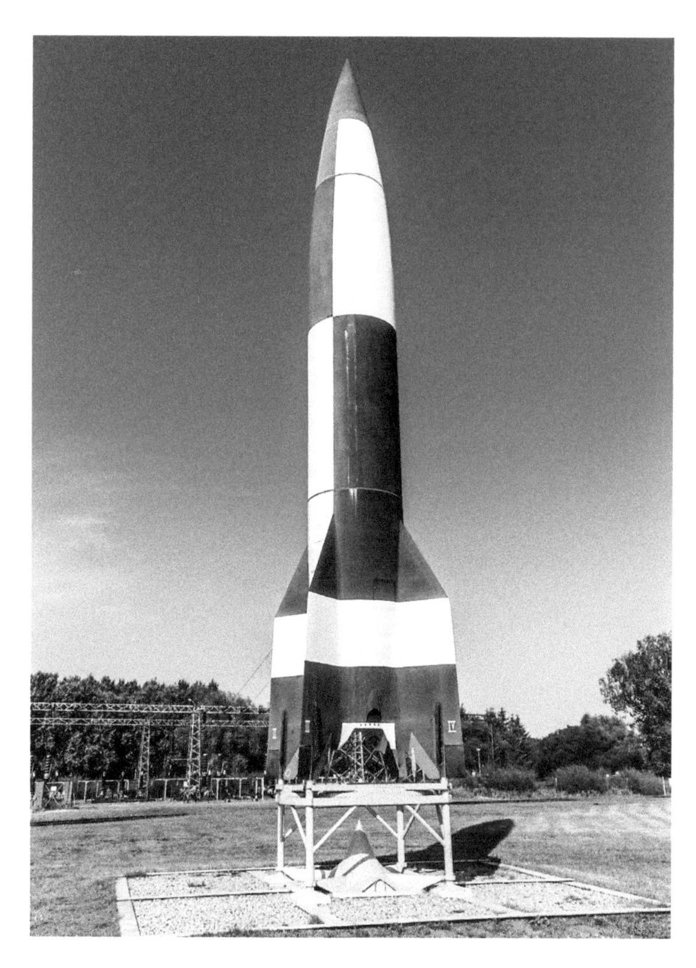

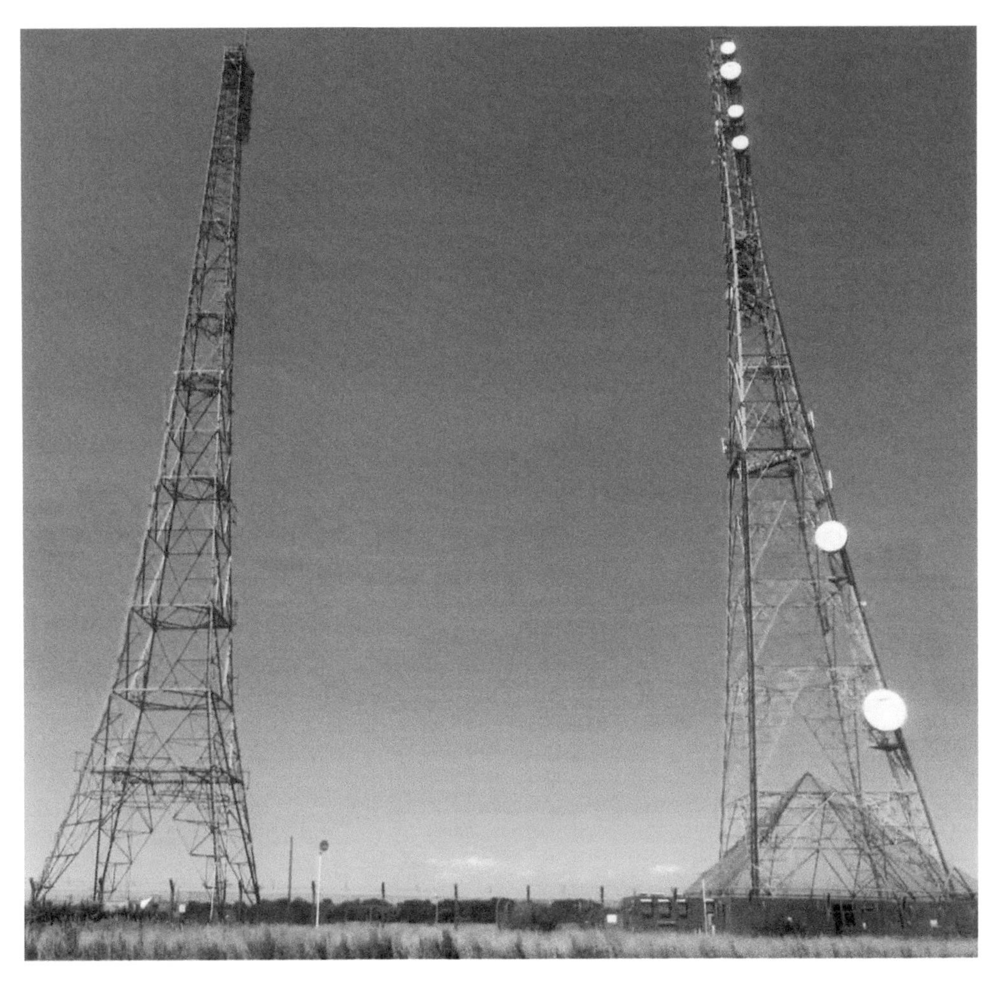

Swingate radar towers, Dover.

The South East Regional War Room was located at Tunbridge Wells (demolished 1997). Its key function following a nuclear strike was to

(a) Collect, collate and submit situation reports to the Central War Room (CWR) at London concerning damage and casualties occurring within the region, the enemy's tactics, and types of weapons used.
(b) Deploy resources to areas suffering damage or casualties beyond the scope of their local resources.
(c) Request and or supply reinforcements from other regions via the CWR.

The County Control Centre was located in Maidstone, staffed by the Number One Group, Royal Observer Corps (ROC), with Local Control Centres established in most large towns. These were connected to each other and a network of ROC ground observation posts and underground monitoring bunkers. The bunkers at Gravesend and Maidstone can be visited, and the remains of many monitoring posts exist across the county.

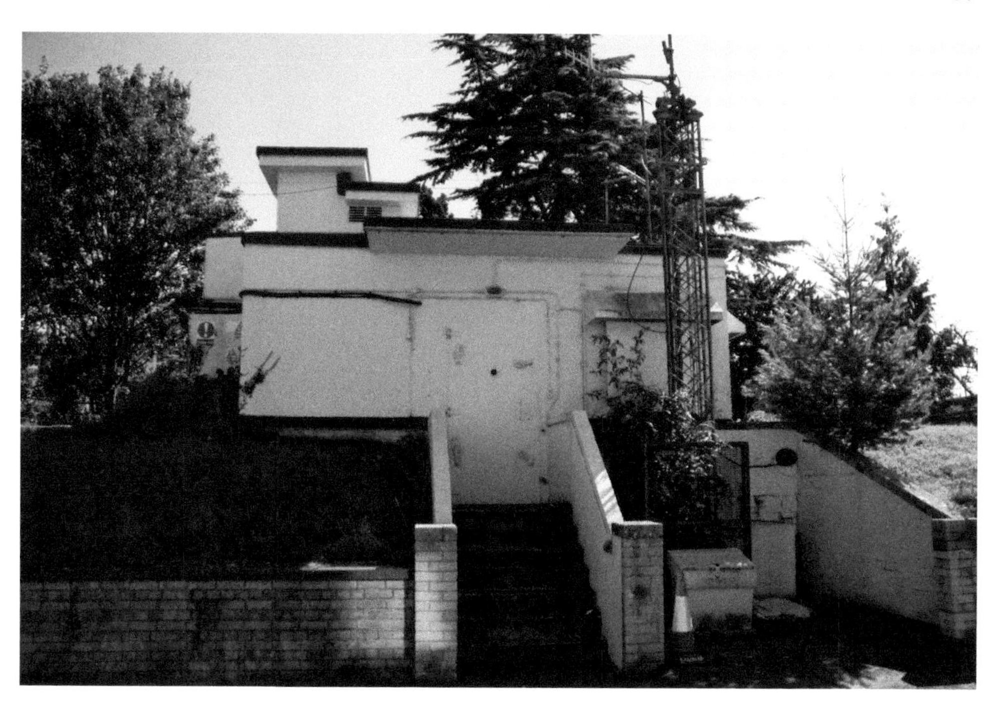

County Control Centre, Maidstone.

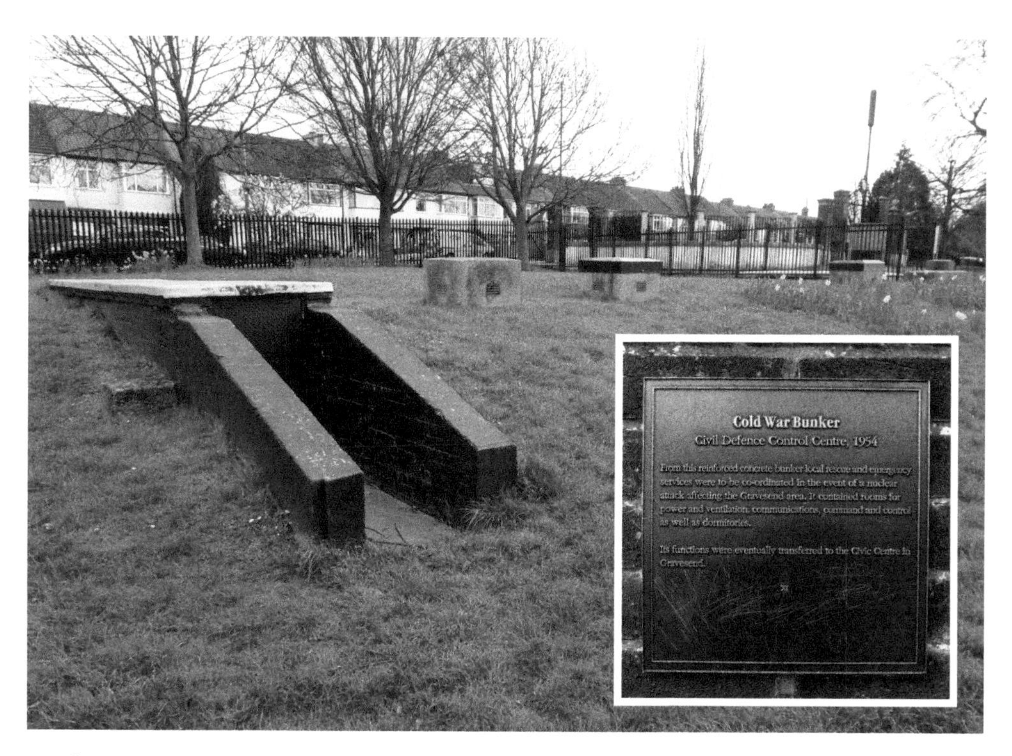

Local Control Centre, Gravesend.

Inset: Local Control Centre plaque.

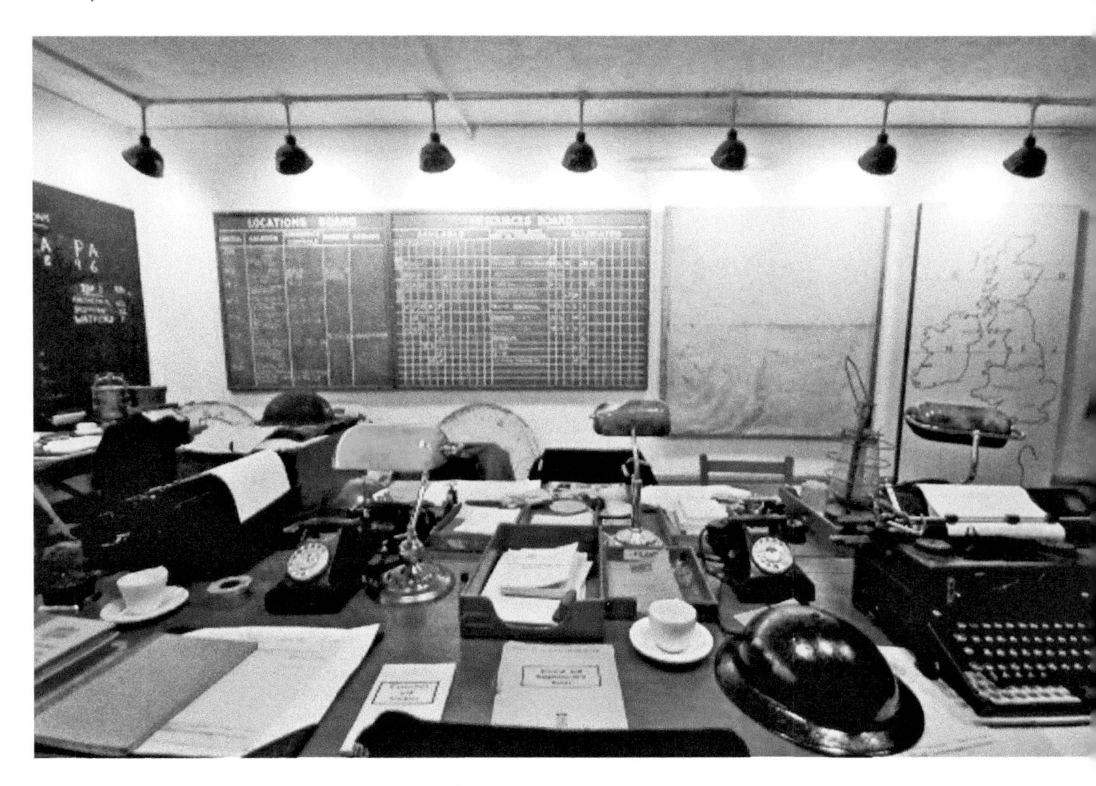

Inside Local Control Centre, Gravesend.

4. More Invaders and Raiders

The year 1914 saw the start of the First World War and the next invasion of the county, and this time the danger was airborne. The Germans' first raid on the UK was made by two seaplanes on 24 December. A bomb intended for Dover Castle landed in a garden near Taswell Street, causing a 10-foot- (30-metre-) wide crater. Despite the damage, there were no casualties, but the residents of Kent would not always be so lucky.

Air raids on Kent continued with varying success, but the most devastating attack came in 1917 when on 25 May, bombers delivered their deadliest payload of the war. Late on Friday afternoon, twenty-three Gotha G 1V heavy bombers were approaching London when stormy weather forced them to turn south. Following the railway to the coast, they headed towards the ports used to convey troops to the western front. At 17.42 hrs they dropped their first bombs on Harvel, Meopham and Luddesdown, causing minimal damage. Further bombs exploded on Ashford Town, Lympne Airfield and the villages of Hythe and Sandgate, killing three civilians and injuring five more.

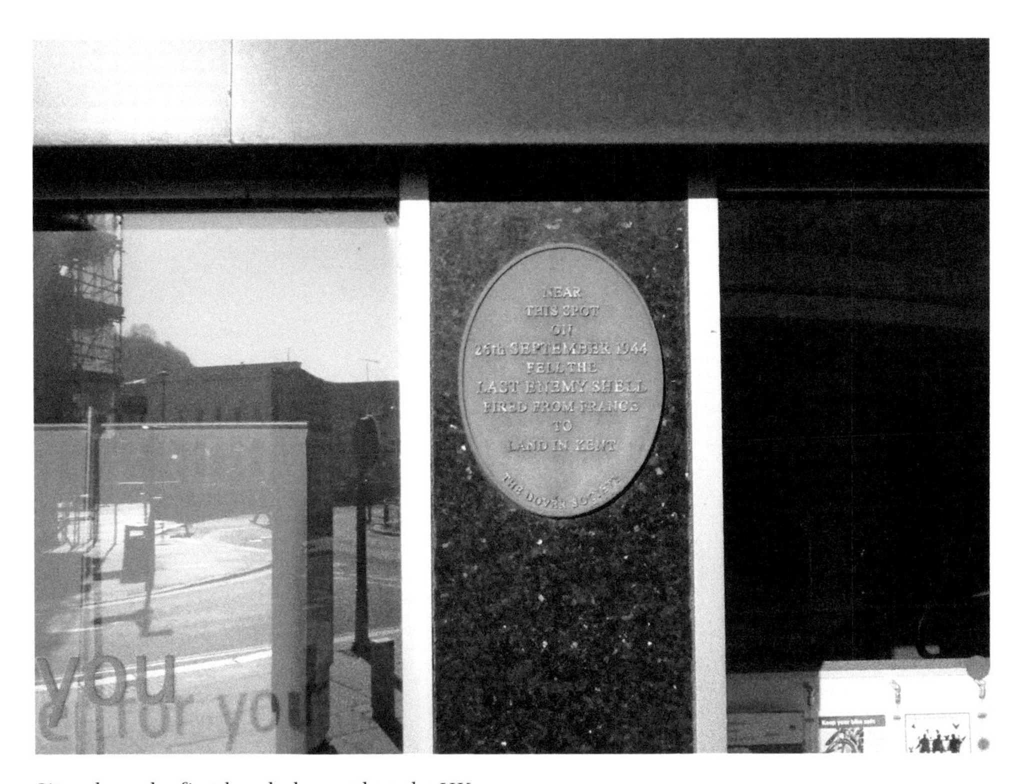

Site where the first bomb dropped on the UK.

Next, they bombed Shorncliffe camp, killing fifteen Canadian soldiers, three civilians and wounding twenty-one others. At 18.00 hrs the squadron released its remaining payload across Folkestone town, killing seventy-five people and injuring 192 others. In Tontine street, one bomb killed sixty-one individuals, the youngest two months old, the eldest eighty. In all the raid claimed the lives of ninety-six men, women and children, many from the same families.

Despite the air-raid warning the attack took residents by surprise, owing to an incident that took place in 1878. Following a collision, 284 crew of the German ironclad warship *Grosser Kurfurst* were killed when it sank off of Folkestone. Local fishing boats rescued eighty-five crew and recovered many more bodies. The people of Folkestone arranged the funerals and supplied the coffins for the dead. They were buried with full military honours at Cheriton Cemetery, where a large monument was erected in their memory. The nation of Germany, grateful to those who rendered assistance, held a special service and bestowed gifts upon them. Until the bombing, residents of Folkestone thought they had been missed out of gratitude for their service to the German sailors in 1878.

As losses mounted, the Germans switched to night-time bombing operations. On 3 September 1917, several hundred naval ratings were sleeping in the barracks at HMS Pembroke, Chatham. Two 100-lb bombs crashed through the roof causing the greatest loss of life in any air raid on Kent: 130 sailors were killed, ninety others wounded.

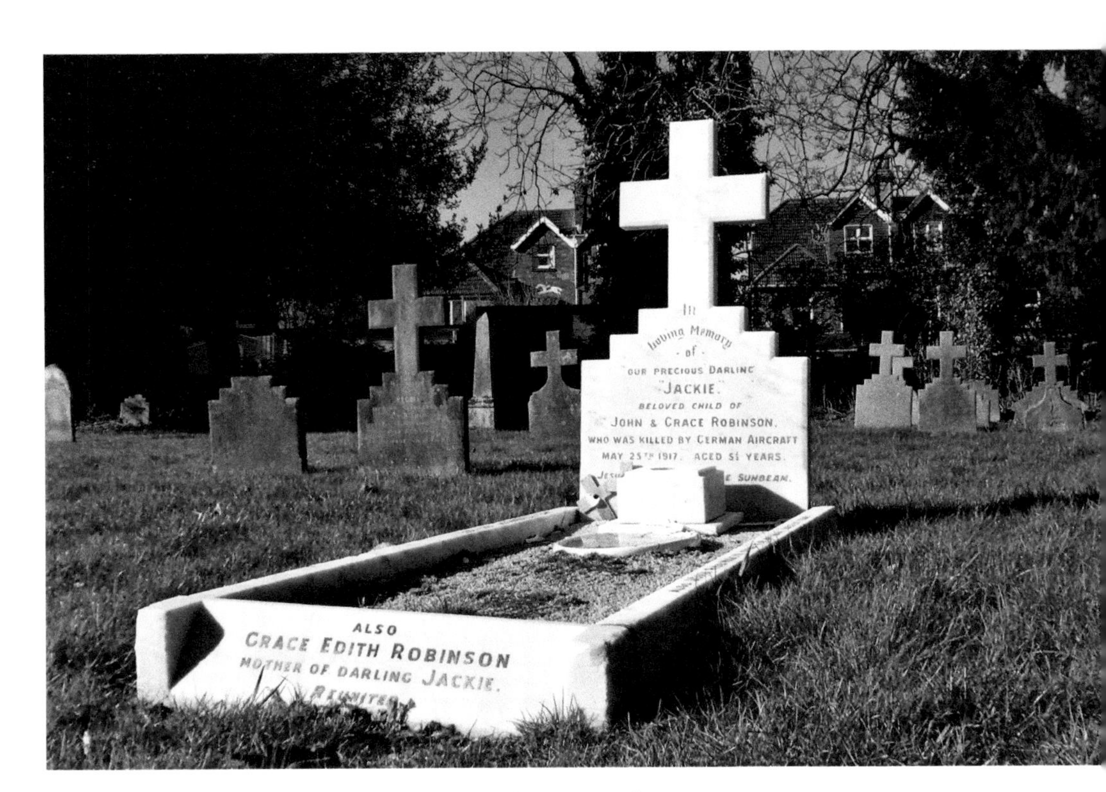

Young victim of Tontine Street bombing, Cheriton Road Cemetery.

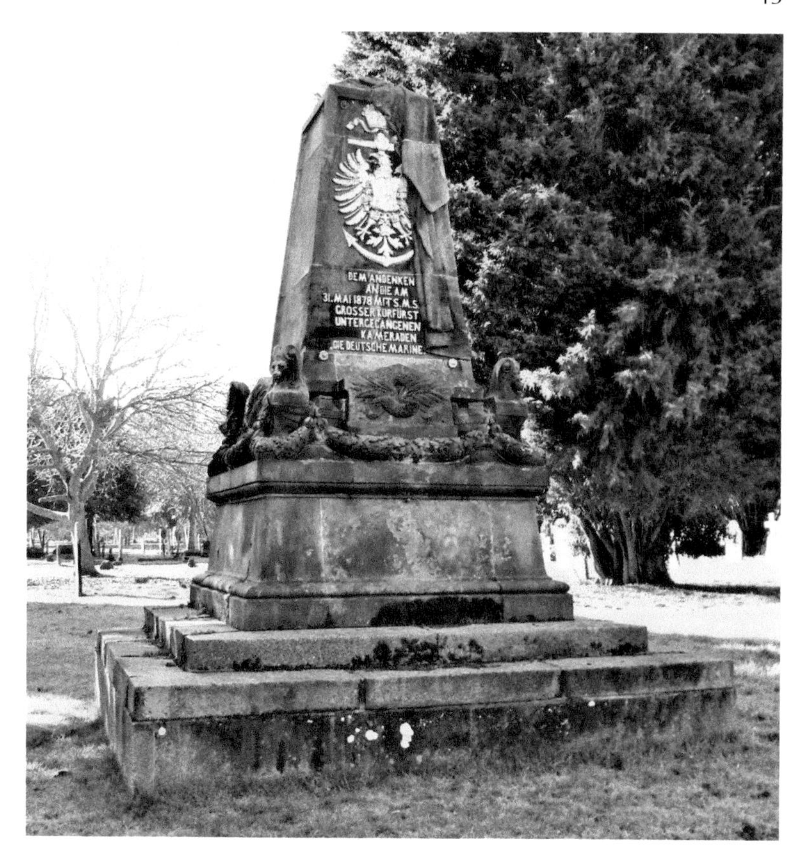

Memorial to German sailors, Cheriton Road Cemetery.

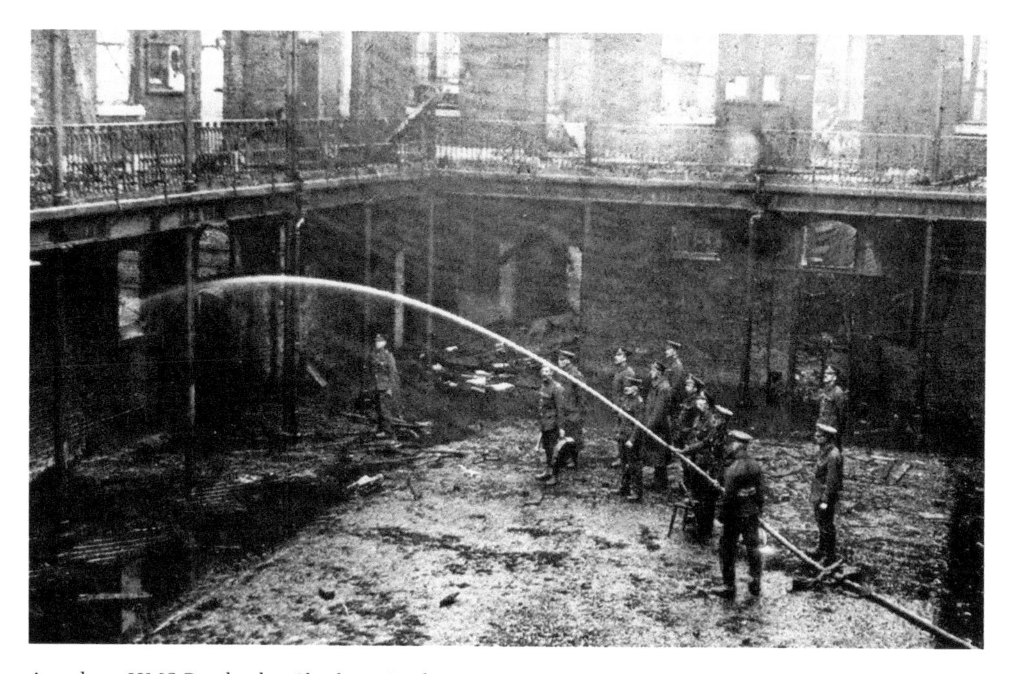

Attack on HMS Pembroke, Chatham Docks, 1917.

Fears of a land invasion persisted, as did air and naval raids, until hostilities ended in 1918. Twenty-two years later in 1940, in the wake of a surprise offensive that saw the Netherlands, Belgium, and France yield to the military forces of Germany, allied soldiers were evacuated from the beaches and harbour at Dunkirk. Once more invasion fears became a reality. Hitler believed Britain would agree peace terms, but if they didn't, he would immediately invade and occupy the nation. Reconnaissance photos taken over Boulogne and Calais in August 1940 showed a large build-up of barges and small craft in the harbours and surrounding areas, fuelling speculation that an invasion was imminent.

Hitler's invasion plan, 'Operation Sea Lion', required air supremacy over southern Britain and the Channel. This would enable the German navy to convey the main invasion fleet towards the south coast. During the summer of 1940, Reichsmarschall Hermann Göring began the Luftwaffe's (German Air Force) all-out campaign to destroy the Royal Air Force (RAF). In July German Bombers attacked shipping to clear the Straits of Dover and in early August, air attacks against British convoys and ports started. By mid-August the German main offensive 'Adlerangriff' (Eagle Attack) had begun. Its aim was to wear down Britain's air defence by targeting airbases, aircraft factories and radar stations in south-east England. Despite being outnumbered, the RAF had superior planes. Between 12 August and 15 September 1940, Kent was at the centre of what became known as the Battle of Britain. Wave after wave of German fighters and bombers attacked and the countryside was littered with the wreckage of aircraft from both sides. The Battle of Britain proved to be one of Britain's most important victories in the Second World War.

Many towns and villages of Kent were bombed during the Second World War, and several attacks were made on Maidstone between July and October 1940, claiming fifty-three lives. The worst day occurred on 27 September 1940 and has since been dubbed 'Black Friday'. German aircraft bombed the town, killing twenty-two people within two minutes.

Roderick Alastair Brook Learoyd, born 5 February 1913 at Folkestone, was awarded the Victory Cross for gallantry in the presence of the enemy during the Battle of Britain, when he led an attack on 12 August 1940 on the Dortmund-Ems Canal, north of Münster, Germany. A vital artery for the German war effort, the canal connected the Ruhr with the North Sea. His citation reads:

> This officer, as first pilot of a Hampden aircraft, has repeatedly shown the highest conception of his duty and complete indifference to personal danger in making attacks at the lowest altitudes regardless of opposition. On the night of 12th August, 1940, he was detailed to attack a special objective on the Dortmund-Ems Canal. He had attacked this objective on a previous occasion and was well aware of the risks entailed. To achieve success it was necessary to approach from a direction well known to the enemy, through a lane of especially disposed antiaircraft defences, and in the face of the most intense point blank fire from guns of all calibres. The reception of the preceding aircraft might well have deterred the stoutest heart, all being hit and two lost. Flight Lieutenant Learoyd nevertheless made his attack at 150 feet, his aircraft being repeatedly hit and large pieces of the main planes torn away. He was almost blinded by the glare of many searchlights at close range but pressed home this attack with the greatest resolution

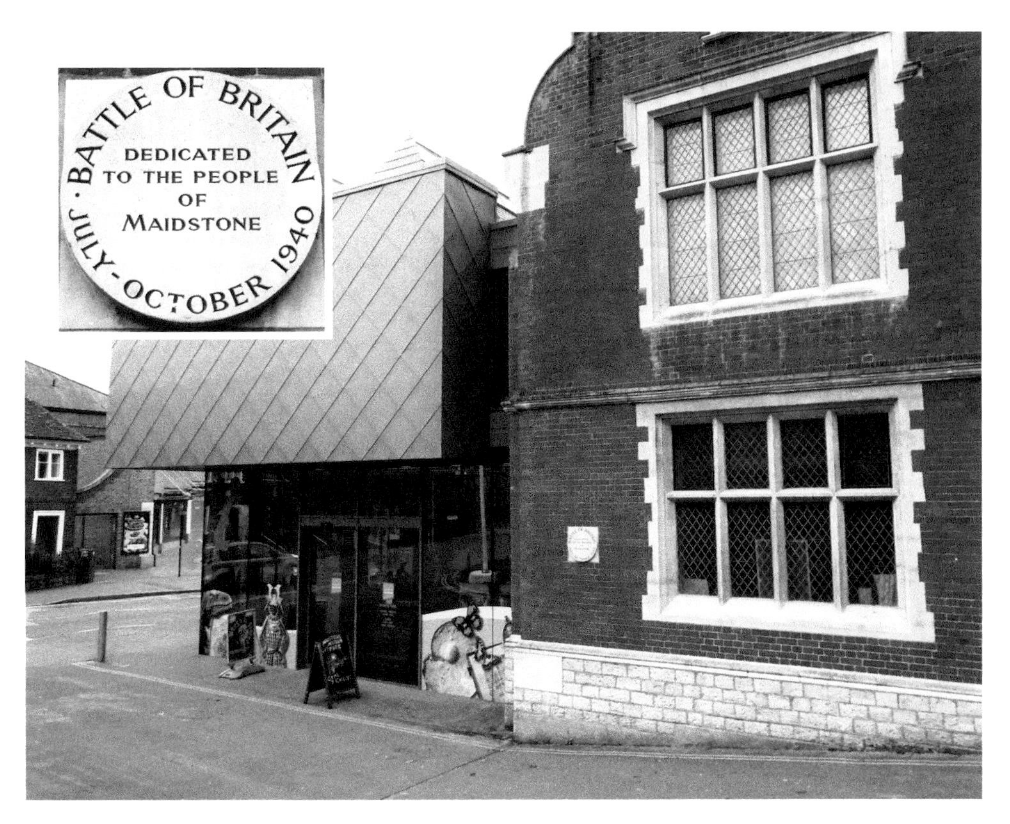

Plaque marking the 1940 attack on Maidstone.

Inset: Image of the plaque.

> and skill. He subsequently brought his wrecked aircraft home and, as the landing flaps were inoperative and the undercarriage indicators out of action, waited for dawn in the vicinity of his aerodrome before landing, which he accomplished without causing injury to his crew or further damage to his aircraft. The high courage, skill and determination, which this officer has invariably displayed on many occasions in the face of the enemy, sets an example which is unsurpassed.

One of Kent's many heritage hubs is the fascinating Battle of Britain Museum at Hawkinge, on the former RAF Hawkinge airfield. The oldest museum dedicated to the battle, it houses the world's largest collection of related artefacts.

Nearby in Hawkinge cemetery lie the remains of ninety-six Second World War casualties, twenty-four of whom, along with fifty-nine Luftwaffe air crew, were killed during the Battle of Britain. Among the German graves rests Gruppenkommandeur Hans-Karl Mayer, a Second World War ace accredited with thirty victories. He disappeared during a test flight over the channel on 16 October 1940 and never returned. His body washed up at Folkestone ten days later. Uniquely, RAF and Luftwaffe crews can be seen buried side by side in the cemetery.

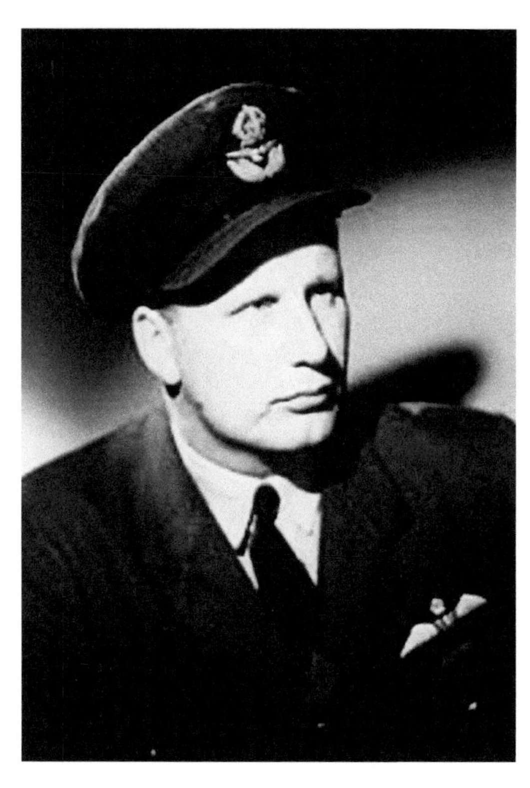

Left: Roderick Alastair Brook Learoyd VC.

Below: Battle of Britain Museum, Hawkinge.

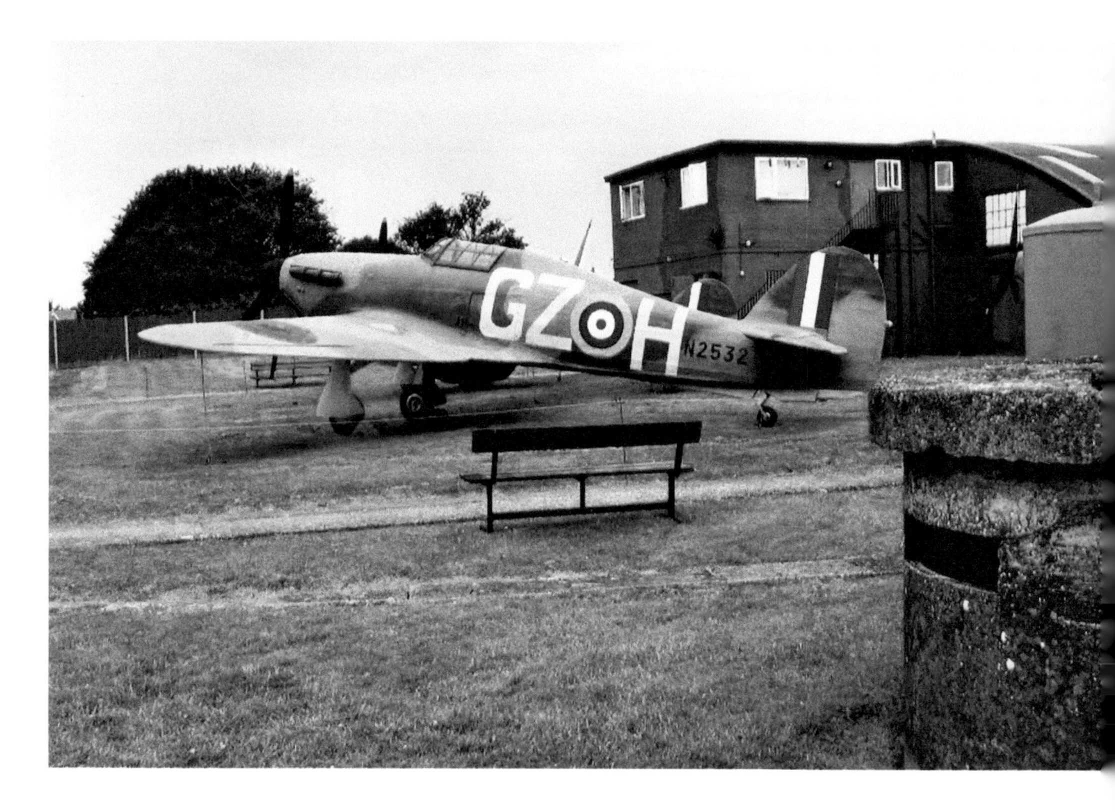

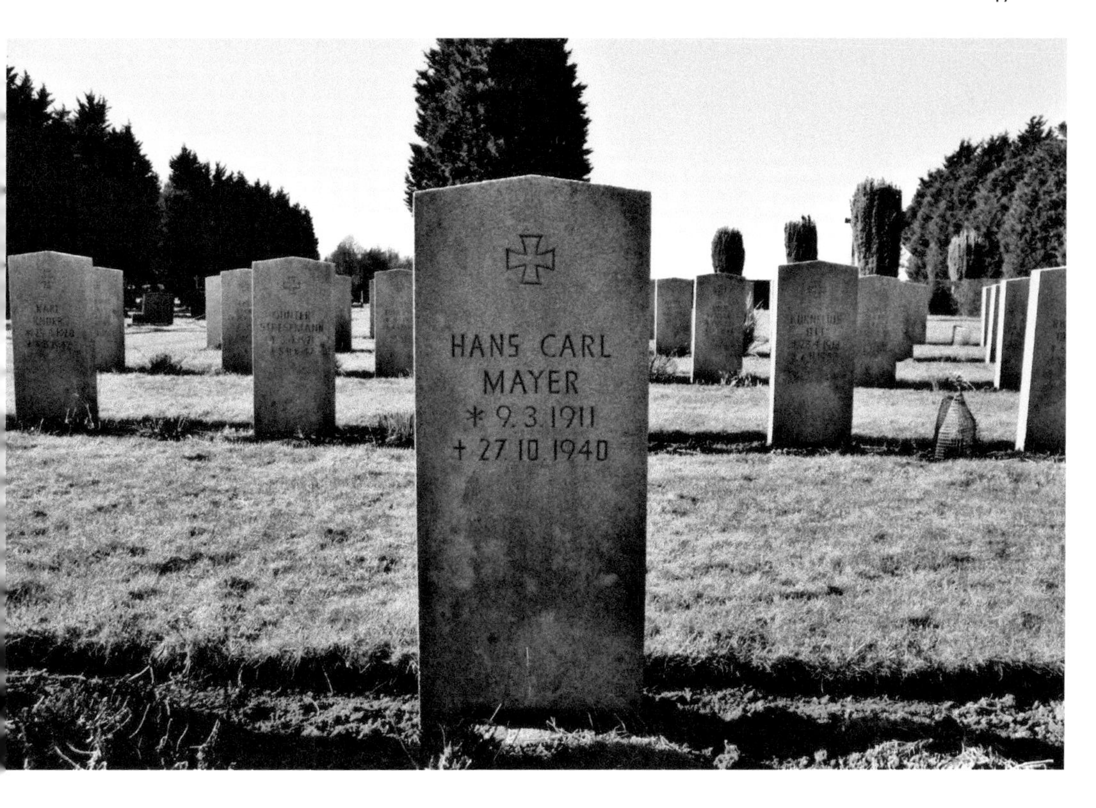

Above: Hans-Karl Mayer's grave.

Right: Hans-Karl Mayer.

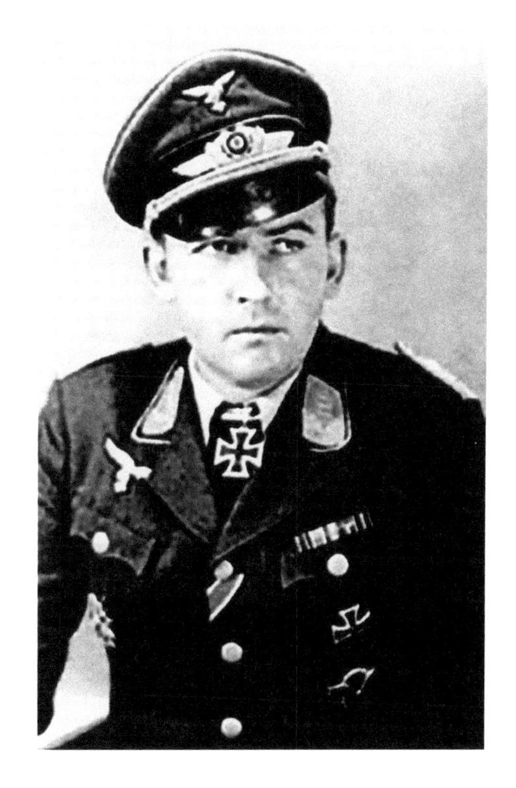

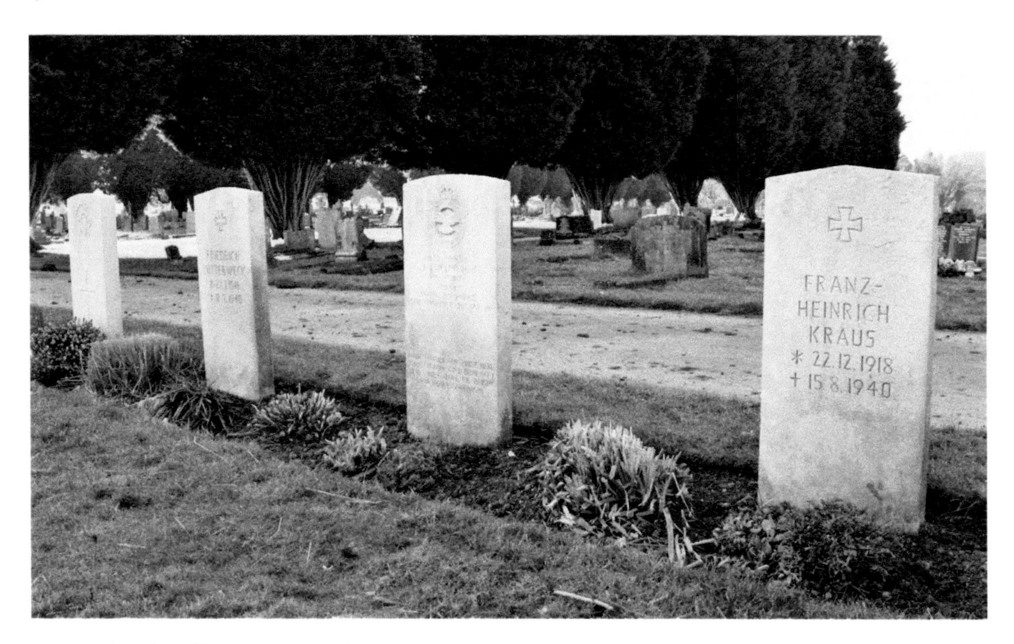

RAF and Luftwaffe airmen, Hawkinge cemetery.

With much of the fighting and air attacks taking place over the coast of south Kent, the Napoleonic tunnels beneath Dover Castle played an important role. They served as headquarters for the joint services evacuation of Dunkirk, and as a military hospital for many airmen. Today, visitors can see the hospital as it was and experience the drama of following a downed pilot as he is rescued from the channel and rushed into the hospital's theatre.

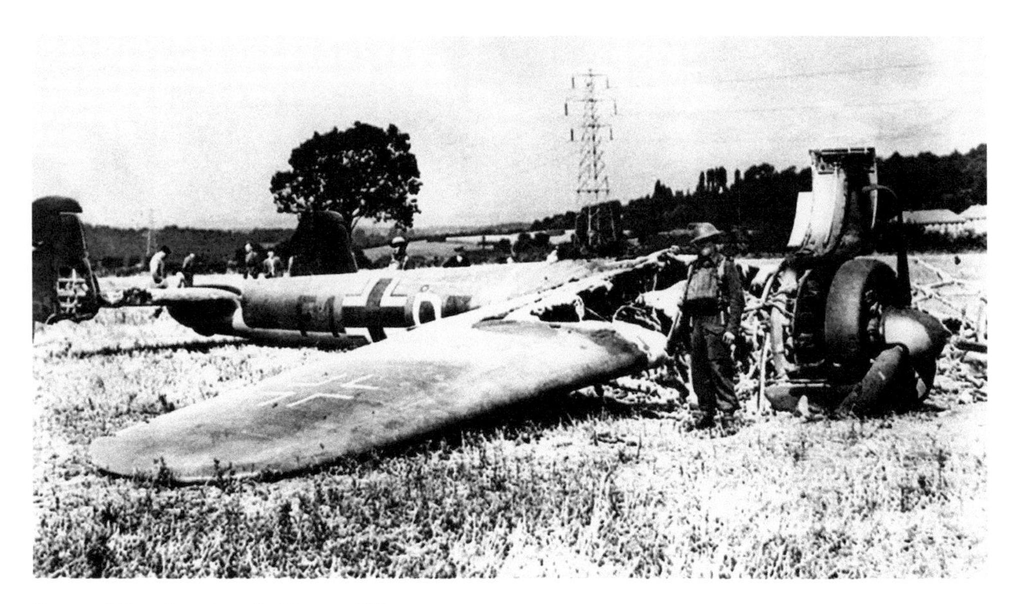

Downed Dornier aircraft, Biggen Hill.

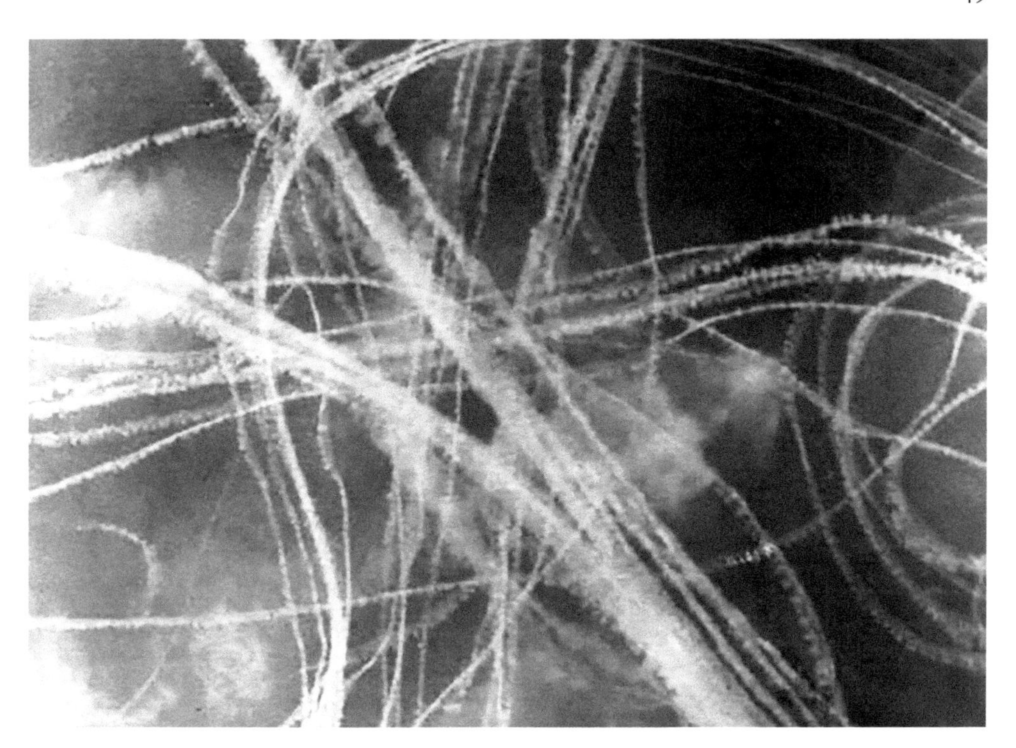

Battle of Britain vapour trails over Kent.

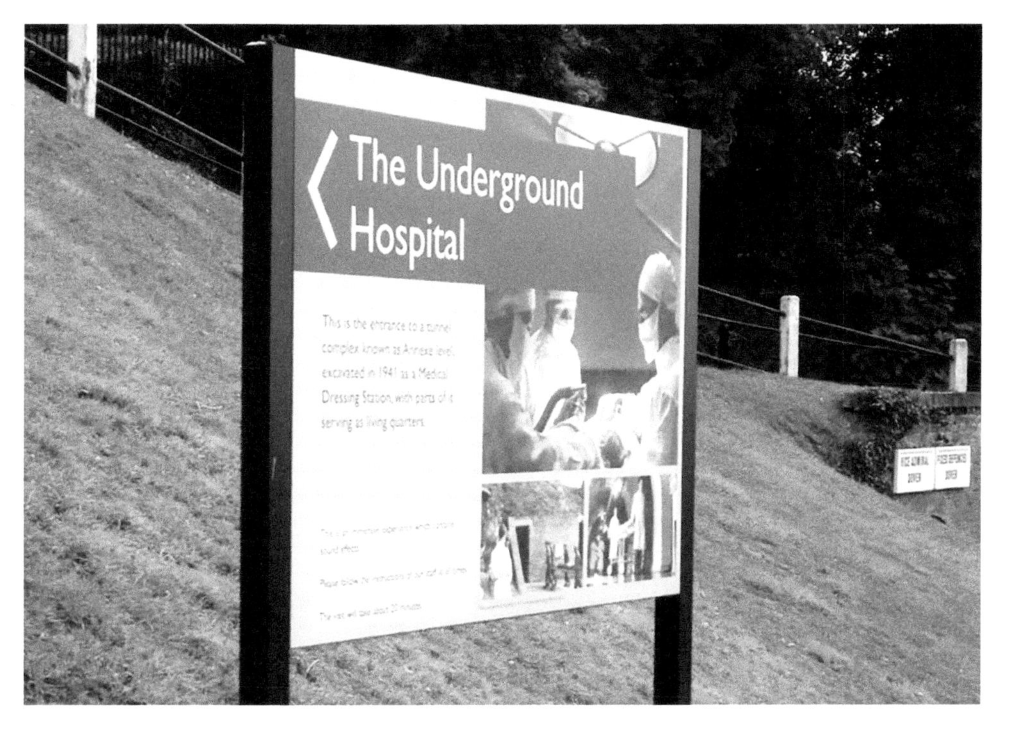

Underground hospital, Dover tunnels.

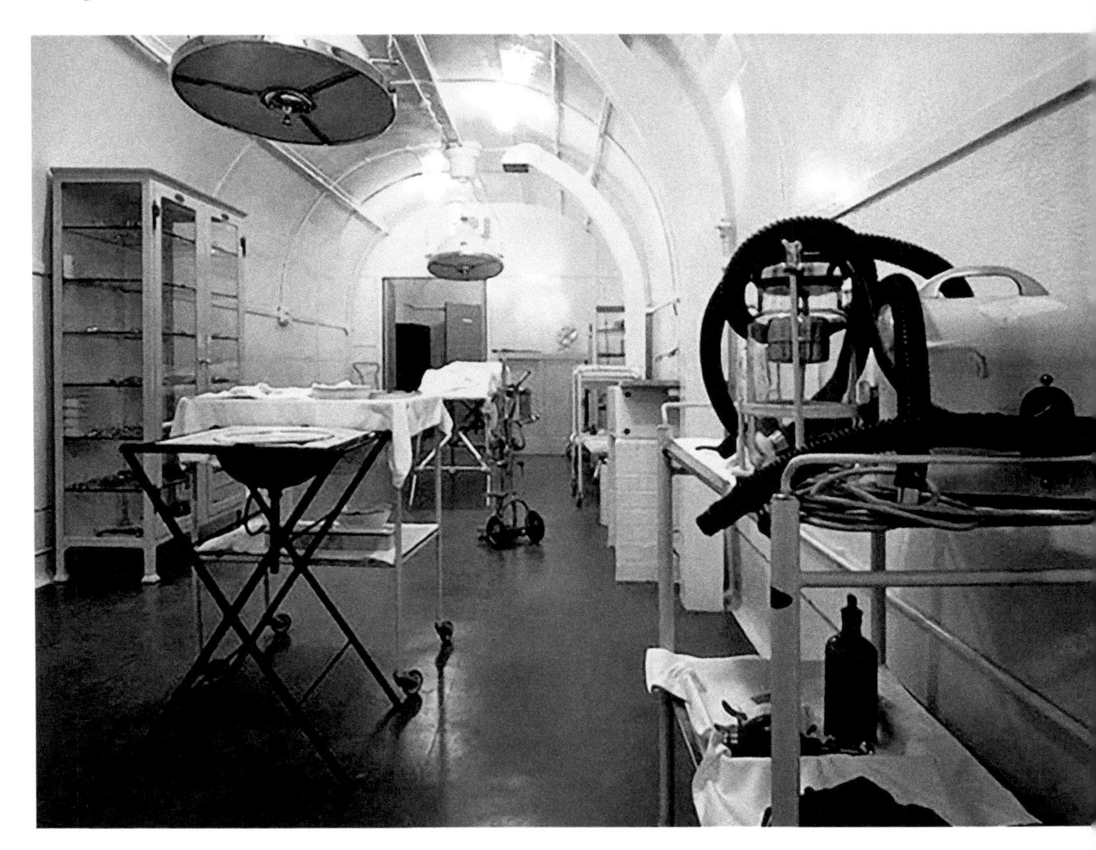

Operating theatre, Dover tunnels.

Because of their proximity to France, the towns and coastal areas of Ramsgate, Folkestone and Dover were relentlessly attacked by German guns in France and were targets for the Luftwaffe's bombing raids. As a result, the area became nicknamed 'Hellfire Corner'. Dover suffered 216 civilian deaths and 10,056 properties were damaged; Folkestone experienced 123 civilian deaths with 14,141 properties damaged. On 24 August 1940 at Ramsgate, 500 bombs were dropped on the town in under five minutes in an attack dubbed 'The Murder Raid'. It was described 'as the world's worst assault from the air' and killed twenty-nine people, destroying seventy-eight houses, leaving 300 unfit for habitation and another 700 damaged.

Casualties would have been much greater had it not been for some foresight and dogged determination by Ramsgate engineer R. D. Brimmell, Mayor A. Bloomfield Courtenay Kempe and the local MP, Captain H. H. Balfour, who constructed a network of protective tunnels below the town. During the First World War, Ramsgate and its surrounding area had been badly bombed. As a result, in 1938, with war on the horizon, Ramsgate Borough Council applied to Westminster to start work on a huge system of underground tunnels. After two refusals, the Home Office granted approval in 1939. The 2.5-mile-long network of tunnels was built in the cliffs under Ramsgate by hand. The tunnels were the most extensive underground public shelter system in the country protecting up to 60,000 people.

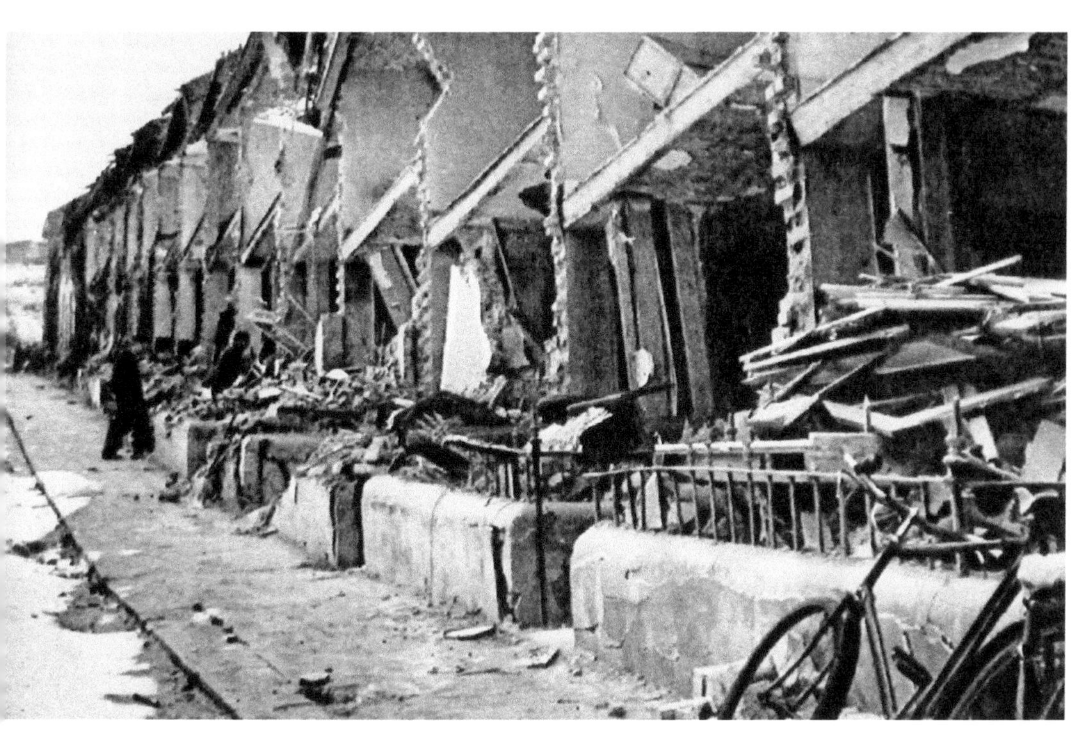

Bomb-damaged street, Dover.

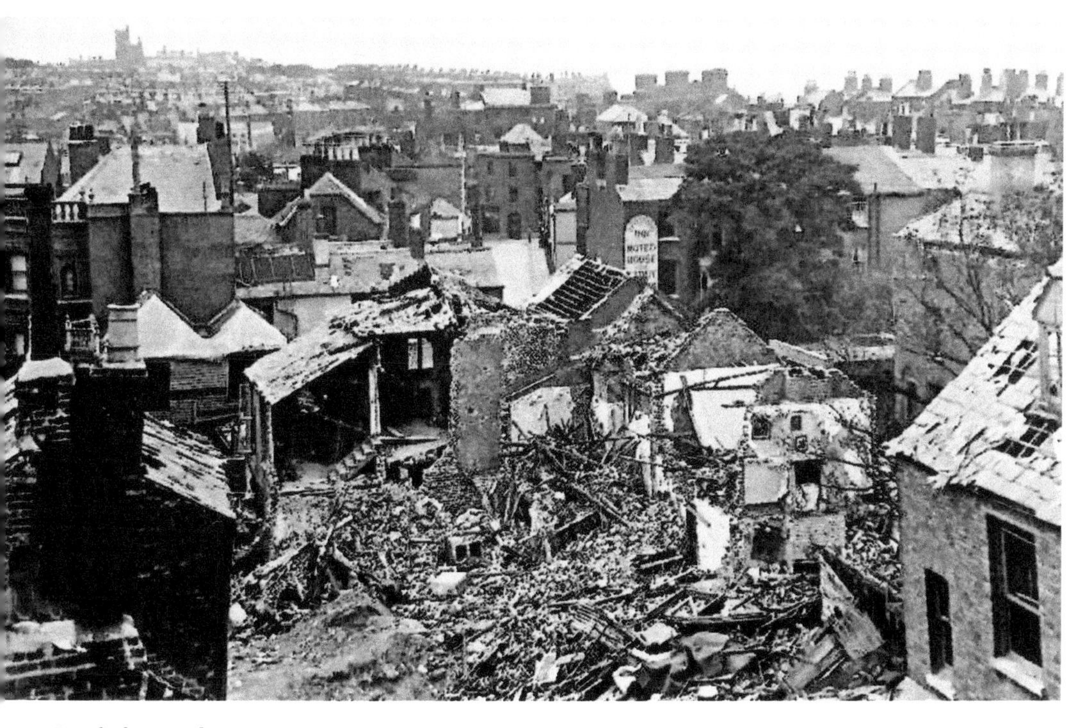

Bomb-damaged street, Ramsgate.

Fitted with street signs and a wide range of facilities, including a barber, concert hall, canteens, shops and other services, the tunnel system even had a hospital. After the war the tunnels were abandoned and sealed. In 1954 plans were made to reuse them for public protection during the Cold War but were never completed. In 2014 they reopened, offering tourists guided tours of the reconstructed shelter and what life was like underground during the war.

The caves at Chislehurst in north Kent provided another subterranean refuge. Covering over 6 hectares, they were located 90 feet (30 metres) below ground and at the height of the Blitz around 15,000 people used them to flee the air raids. A weekly rent of sixpence for an adult and thruppence for a child was charged and people would enter the caverns every evening by 7 p.m. and leave after 7 a.m. the following morning. Long-term residents brought their own mattresses, beds and chairs and, like the Ramsgate Tunnels, their amenities included a cinema, barber, three canteens and a cave chapel consecrated by the Bishop of Rochester. There was also a functional hospital, staffed by a Red Cross doctor and two nurses serving seven wards and an isolation unit. They closed when the war ended and reopened for tours in the 1960s, which continue today.

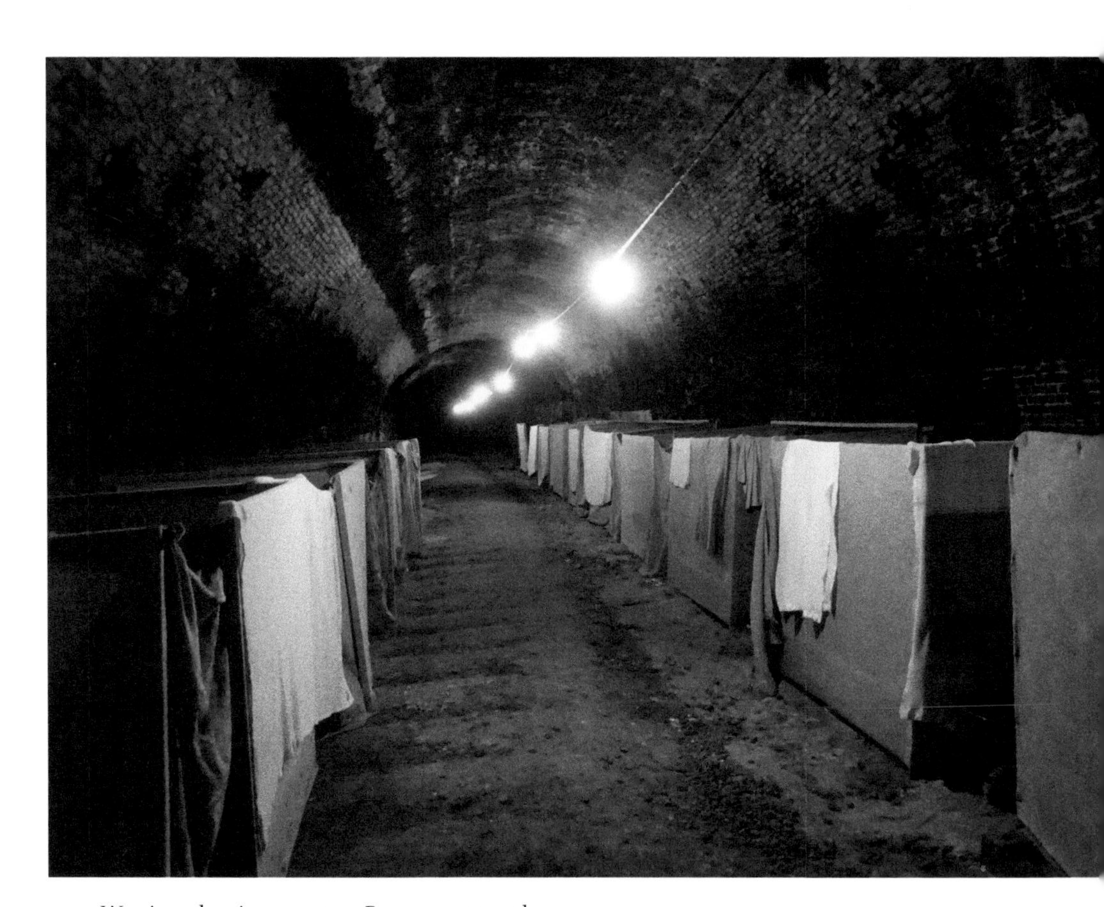

Wartime sleeping quarters, Ramsgate tunnels.

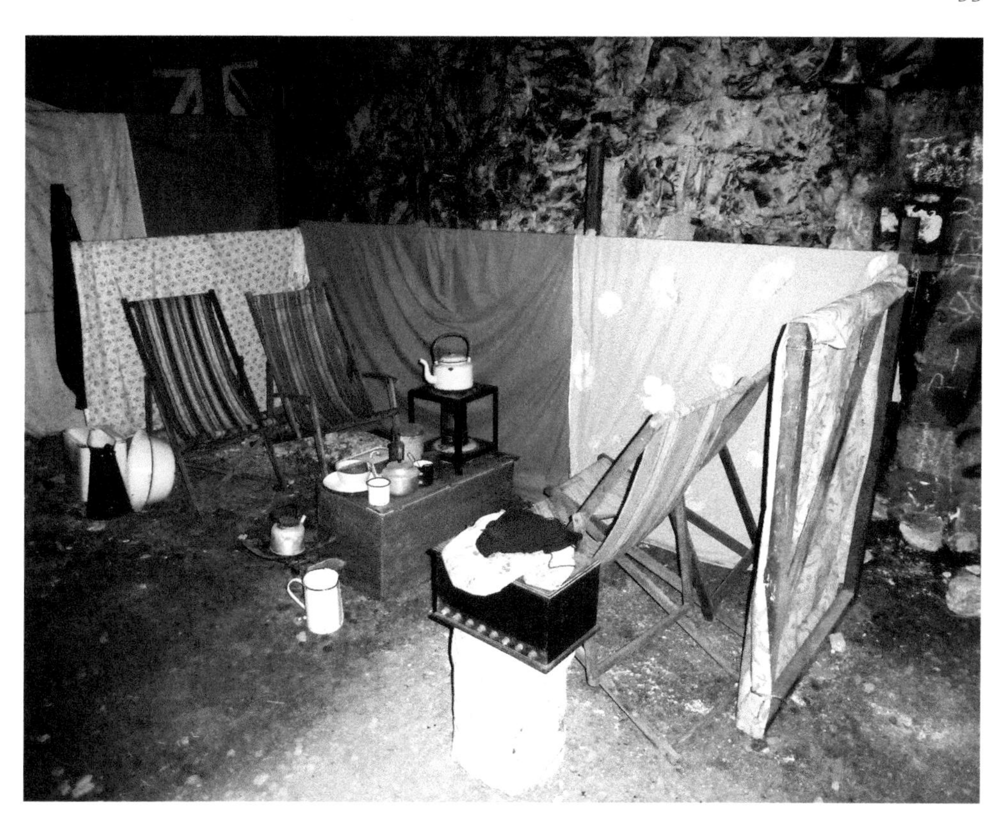

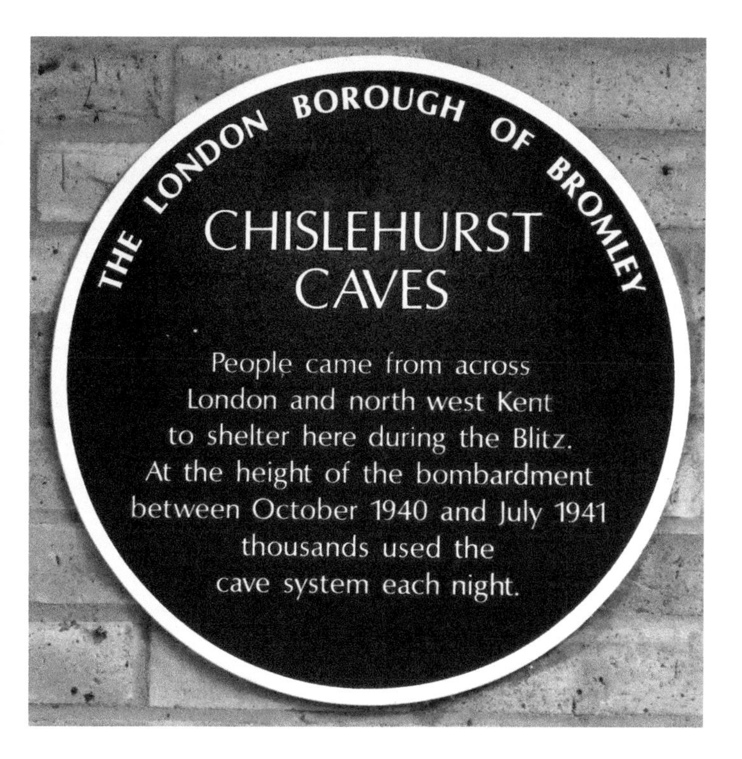

Above: Home comforts, Ramsgate tunnels.

Right: Plaque, Chislehurst Caves.

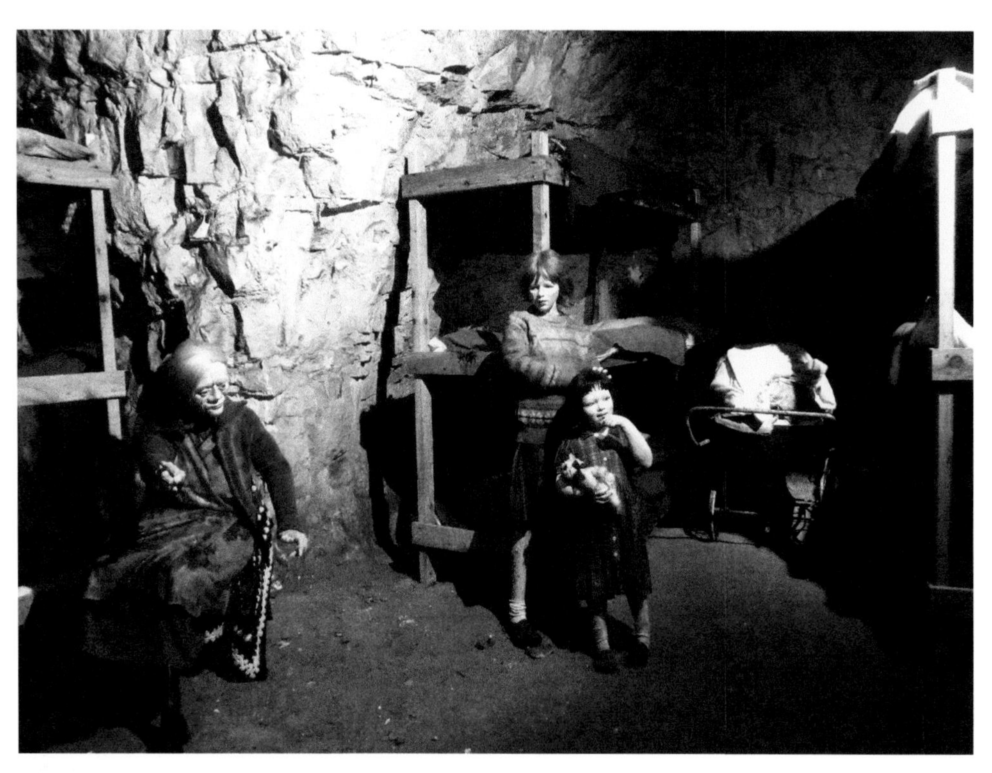

Second World War dormitory, Chislehurst Caves.

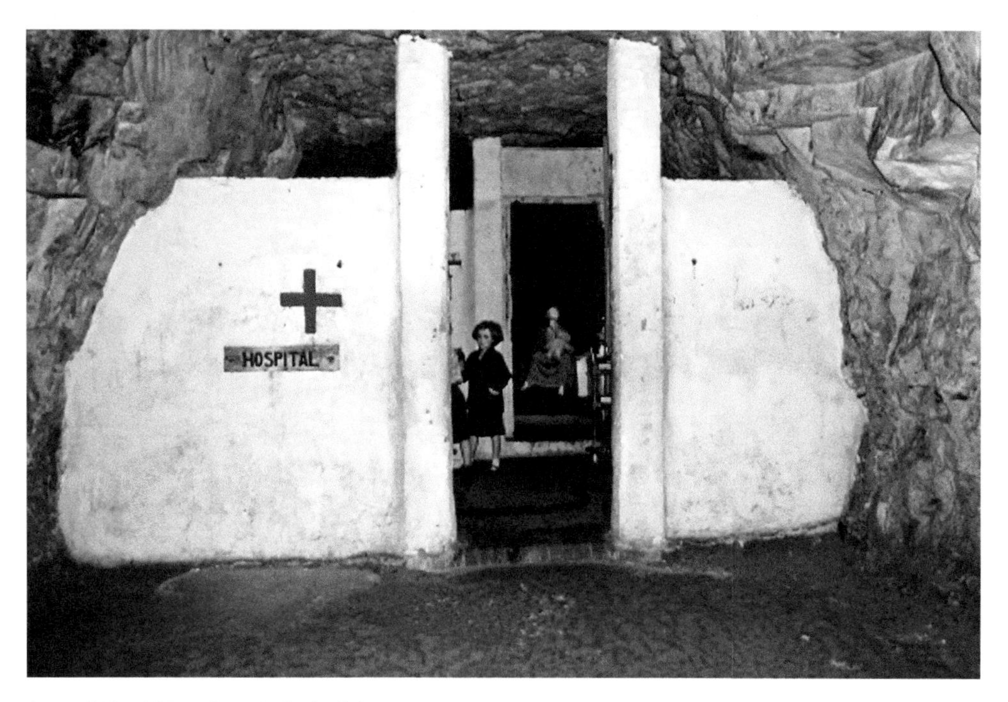

Second World War hospital, Chislehurst Caves.

The final raids on Kent came from Hitler's new long-range reprisal weapons, including the V-1 flying bomb or 'Doodlebug', V-2 rocket and the V-3 cannon. Once more Kent was on the front line, with RAF gunners and balloon handlers fighting hard to limit the damage caused on the ground. The first V-1 was launched just days after D-Day 'Operation Overlord' on 4 June 1940, the allied invasion of Normandy, France. Hitler's reprisal made Kent the most attacked county. Around 2,400 V-1s landed along 'Bomb Alley', the nickname given by the people of Kent to land running from the Thames Estuary down to Dover.

While the V-1 emitted a distinctive throbbing noise as it approached its target, the V-2 was a far more terrifying weapon, arriving with no warning and devastating consequences. The last ever V-2 landed in Kent on 27 March 1945, killing one person, and the last V-1 struck two days later. Fortunately, Germany's use of the V-3 cannon, capable

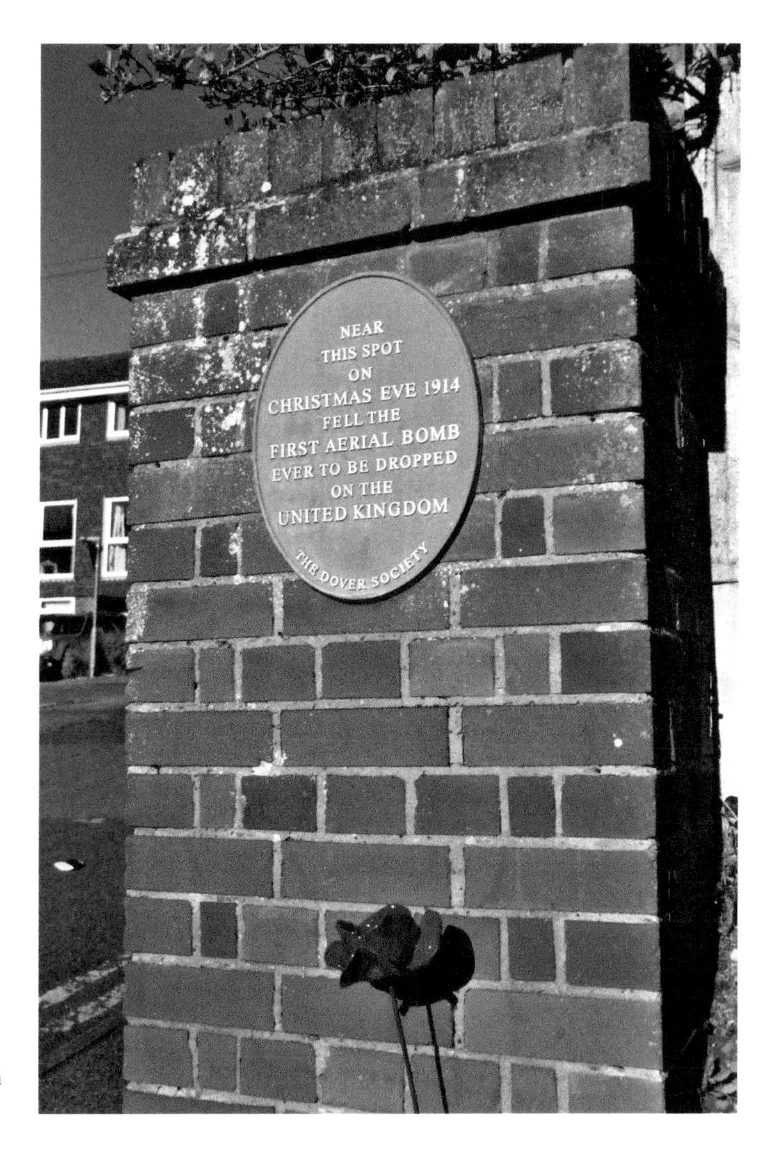

Site of the last German shell to fall on Kent.

of hitting a target over 100 miles (165 km), was curtailed by effective RAF bombing. This derailed attempts to construct the weapon until ground troops arrived from Normandy to capture them. The last shell to land on Kent was fired from France by a railgun that landed near Castle Street, Dover, on 26 September 1944.

The next time a foreign army attacked Kent was 25 September 1975 when terrorists attacked the county. The Provisional Irish Republican Army (PIRA), targeting military personnel from the Royal Engineers barracks at Maidstone, planted a bomb under a car outside the Hare & Hounds pub, Lower Boxley Road. A serving soldier and former Northern Ireland veteran, looking for someone who had left their coat in the bar, spotted the device and raised the alarm. The pub was cleared, nearby homes were evacuated, and roads sealed off. Thirty minutes later at 22.00 hrs, the bomb exploded, wrecking the car and damaging the pub, but no one was injured. The explosion was the seventh in Britain within a month and the bombers were eventually caught following an armed siege in Balcombe Street, London.

The IRA attacked Kent again on 22 September 1989 when they bombed the Royal Marines music school barracks at Deal. The blast destroyed a three-storey building, killing eleven marines and injuring another twenty-one. Despite the soldiers being ceremonial musicians and trainees, the IRA declared the music school a legitimate target, provoking public outrage and condemnation. To date, nobody has been brought to justice for the bombing.

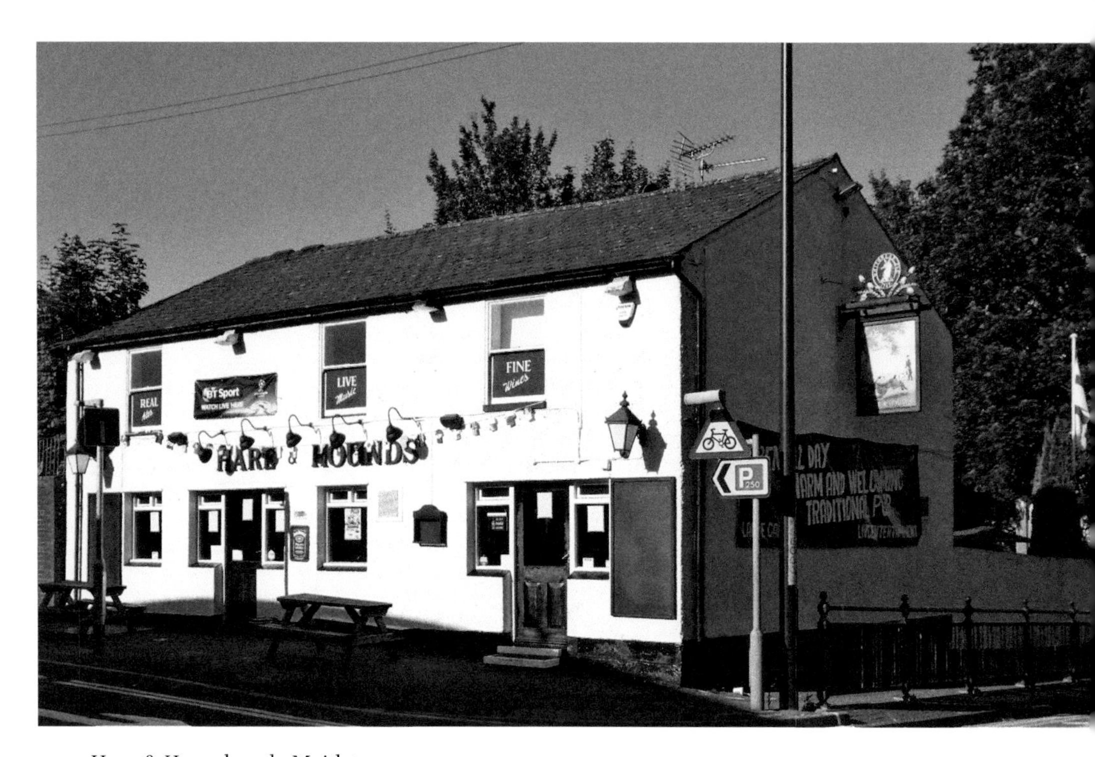

Hare & Hounds pub, Maidstone.

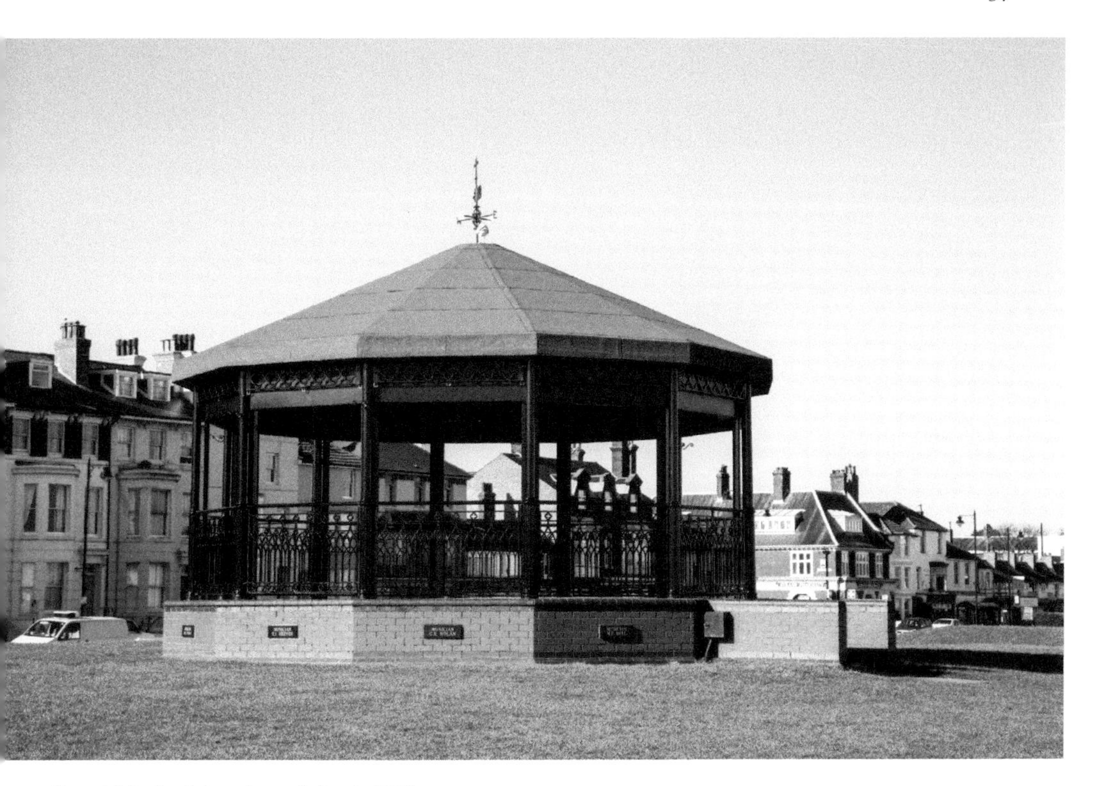

Royal Marine's bandstand, Deal. (DT.)

5. The Royal Dockyards

Alfred, King of Wessex between 871–901, built England's first royal fleet of nine ships in response to sustained attacks by Danish raiders. Before then there had been no dedicated defence capability for coastal waters. Early attempts to create a seafaring force came during the reign of Edward the Confessor in 1004–66, who created the maritime institution of the Cinque Ports, dubbed the 'Cradle of the Royal Navy'. The original confederation of coastal towns was Dover, Hastings, Romney, Hythe and Sandwich, and later in the thirteenth century, Rye and Winchelsea were included. Established to oversee military activity and trade at the Cinque Ports, the reigning monarch appointed Lord Wardens who held baron status and the right to attend the king's parliament. When required they provided ships and men to engage pirates and enemy attackers, and in return they received many financial, political and royal privileges and honours.

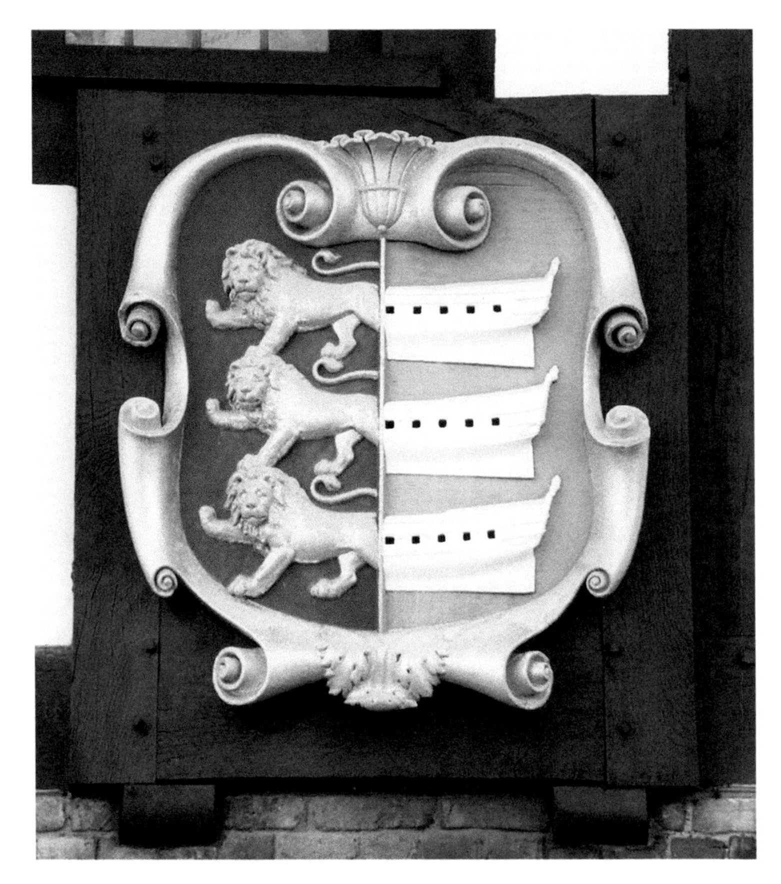

Cinque Ports emblem, Guildhall, Sandwich.

The confederation had its own distinctive heraldic emblem: the front half of a lion joined to the back of a ship repeated three times vertically. The symbol appears in several of the Cinque Port towns' coats of arms and can be seen in various forms throughout their boroughs. By the reign of Queen Elizabeth I, a combination of natural forces – weakening coastal defences and shifting sandbanks – led to harbours silting up and rivers changing course, resulting in their decline. Another marked factor was a military and commercial need for larger ships and bigger, deeper ports.

Chatham's position as a naval dockyard arose following King Henry VIII's use of the River Medway as a place of safe anchorage for his fleet. The River Medway provided ideal conditions and superior facilities to drop anchor than other rivers, ports and docks in the region. By 1547 Chatham became a major base for Queen Elizabeth I's navy. Designated a Royal Naval Dockyard in 1568, it launched its first warship, the *Sunne*, in 1586. Chatham established its military importance over the next 400 years, playing a pivotal role in defending the realm. The dockyard ensured Britain's maritime supremacy by building, repairing and refitting warships of all classes.

Advances in science and technology, leading to changes in shipbuilding, naval practices and warfare, were constant. By 1613 the dockyard became too small, causing it to move a short distance downriver to the site of today's Historic Dockyard. It continued to expand to accommodate developments in dockyard manufacturing processes such as timber, iron and steel working, and rope and sail making. The dockyard became an industrialised military complex spanning 400 acres and employing around 10,000 workers. Today many of the later eighteenth- and nineteenth-century buildings form part of the dockyard's maritime museum.

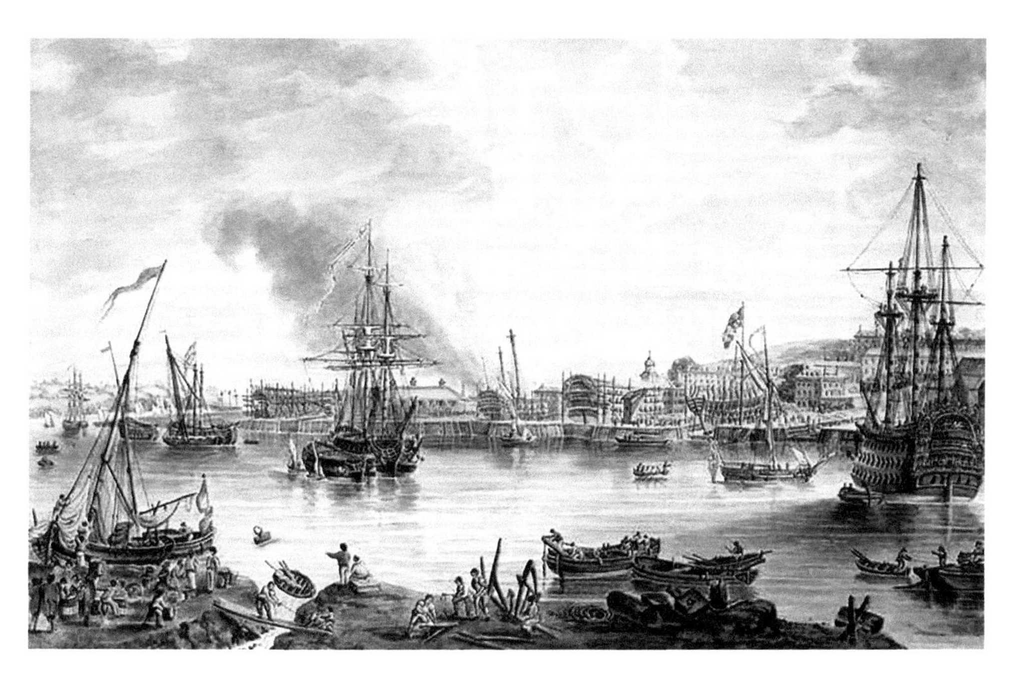

HMS *Royal George* and HMS *Queen Charlotte*, Chatham Dockyard, 1790.

After its closure in 1984, the site was separated into three areas. Area one became a commercial port while area two became new residencies and leisure facilities. Area three, an expanse of 84 acres, was transferred to the Chatham Historic Dockyard Trust. This is now a visitor attraction showcasing Kent's premier maritime military heritage.

Among the exhibits and activities are forty-seven Scheduled Ancient Monuments and other listed buildings, including memorials and three historic warships, a Victorian sloop, the HMS *Gannet*, a Second World War Destroyer, the HMS *Cavalier*, and the last Royal Navy warship built at Chatham Dockyard, the HM Submarine *Ocelot*. The ropery was the longest brick building of its day, over 1,100 feet, (340 metres), and is still in use today, while the Commissioner's House, erected in 1704, remains Britain's oldest surviving royal naval building. Many famous ships were built and launched during its service, including Lord Nelson's HMS *Victory*; HMS *Temeraire*; HMS *Achilles* (1863), the first iron warship to be built in a Royal Dockyard; and HMS *Africa* (1905), the last battleship to be built at the yard. Following the Second World War, focus moved to building and refitting submarines. The Canadian submarine *Okanagan* was the last boat ever to be built at the dockyard. Today it remains an outstanding example of a naval industrial complex that has spanned the age of sail and the age of steam.

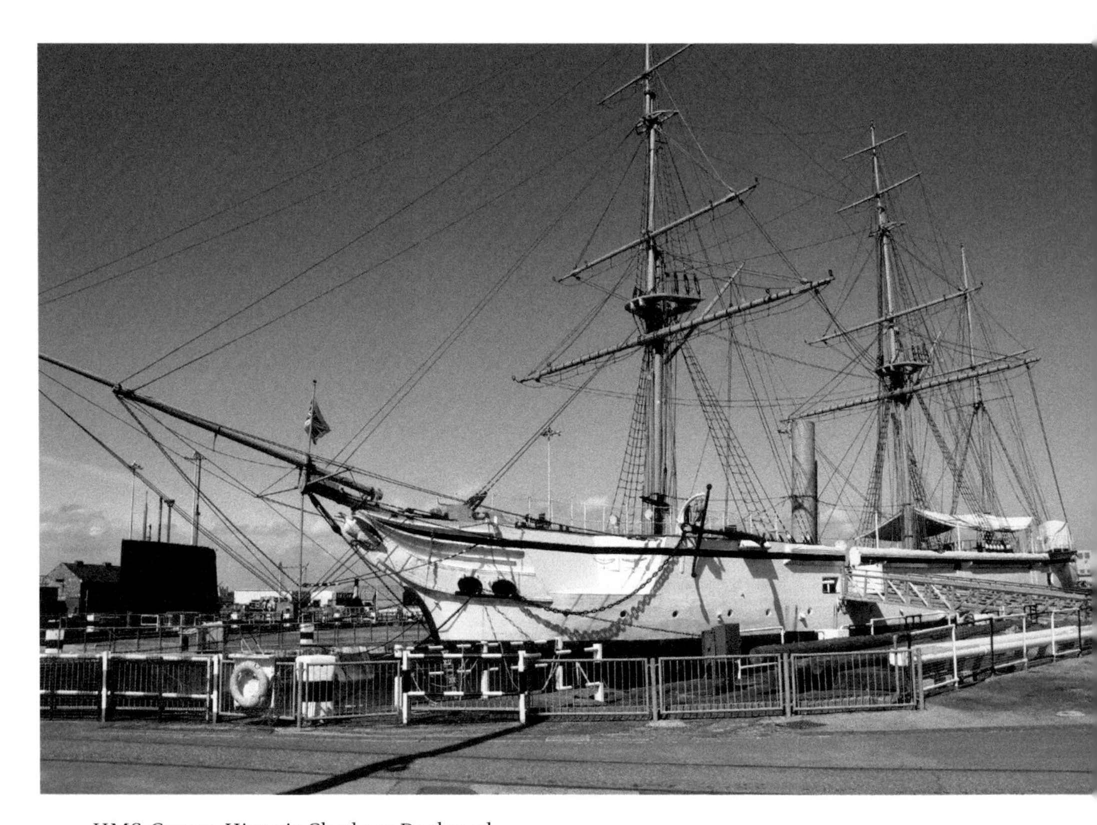

HMS *Gannet*, Historic Chatham Dockyard.

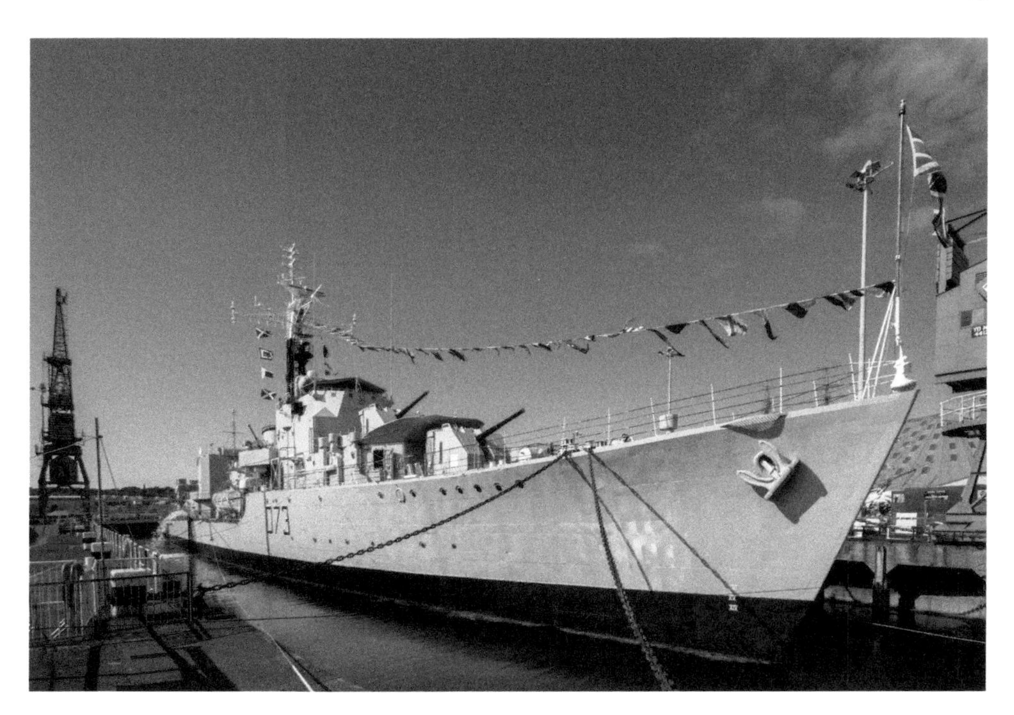

HMS *Cavalier*, Historic Chatham Dockyard.

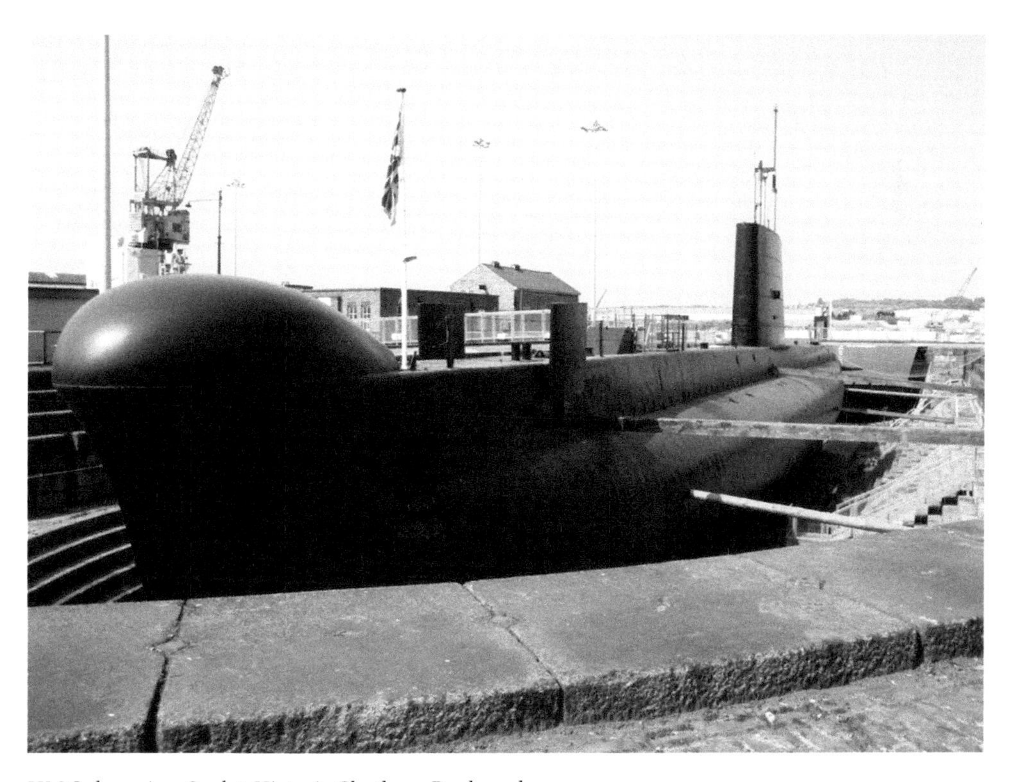

HM Submarine *Ocelot*, Historic Chatham Dockyard.

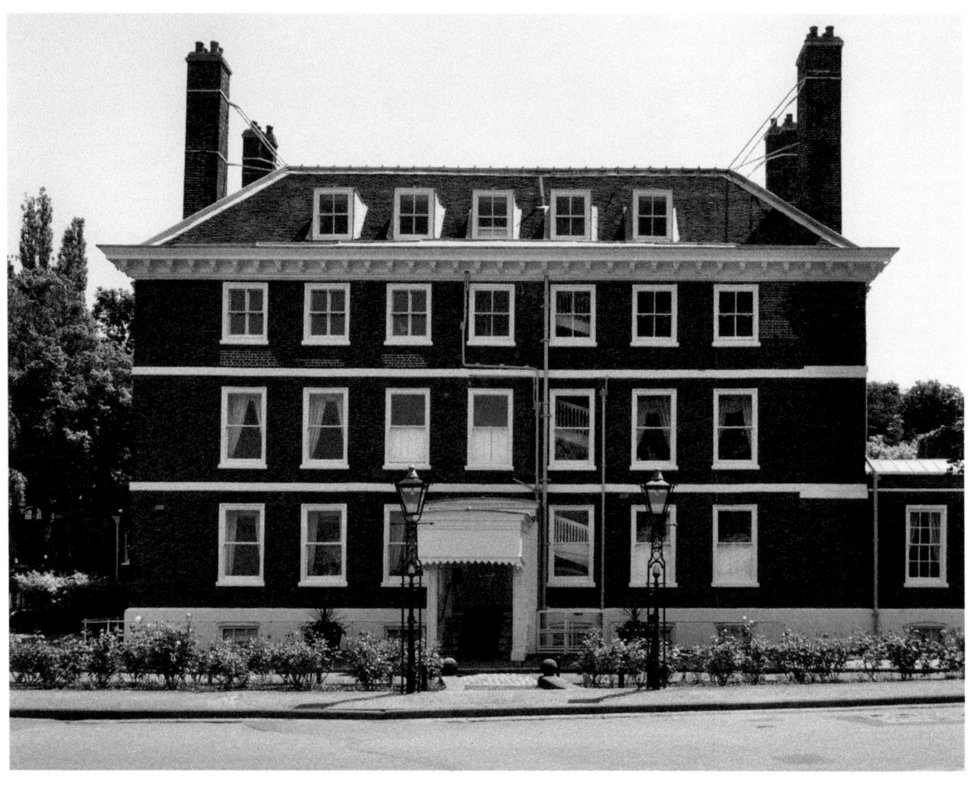

Commissioner's House, Historic Chatham Dockyard.

Kent's other Royal Navy dockyard, Sheerness, dates back to the reign of King Charles II, who ruled England, Scotland and Ireland from 1660 to 1685. It was established in 1665 and served as a support yard for Chatham Dockyard, storing and refitting smaller ships. Before Sheerness Dockyard was built, Garrison Point Fort stood on the site, defending the entrance to the River Medway. The incomplete fort was destroyed in June 1667 during an attack by the Dutch fleet. It was rebuilt with more robust defences, including a line of heavy cannons and a battery of artillery gunners who were permanently stationed there.

The dockyard built small ships, frigates and other smaller vessels from 1691. By 1840 it had expanded to 60 acres as Chatham Dockyard could not help with the repair and maintenance of steam-powered ships based in the Thames Estuary. Sheerness was further adapted to receive larger steamships. The second mast house was converted into an engineering foundry and fitting shop and No. 1 and No. 3 Docks were lengthened to accommodate the new ships. In 1854, a new steam factory was built in the dockyard and by 1868 it employed just under 500 men and boys. The absence of a nearby town created difficulties for workers looking for accommodation, and the docks receiving water and other supplies. This curtailed expansion, preventing it from taking a prominent place in naval history. Despite some improvements in facilities, by 1960 the lack of effective victualling amenities became too problematic and in March 1960 the dockyard closed, becoming a commercial port.

6. Aviation, Airfields and Air Personnel

Kent's association with military aviation dates back to the 1880s when the Royal Engineers (RE) moved the School of Ballooning and the Balloon Equipment Store from Woolwich Arsenal, London, to the School of Military Engineering, Chatham. There they conducted experiments with observation balloons and by the end of 1883 had produced their first balloon, the Heron. Following continued successes in balloon development and design, the school moved to larger quarters in Aldershot, Hampshire, in 1892. In February 1904, Samuel Cody (a pioneer aviator who would in 1908 complete the first UK powered aeroplane flight) joined the RE No. 2 Balloon School at Lydd Camp, Romney Marsh, and taught the army how to build and fly his man-lifting kites. His design, 'The Bat', climbed as a kite but fell as a glider and was viewed as a more stable choice to the balloon in strong winds.

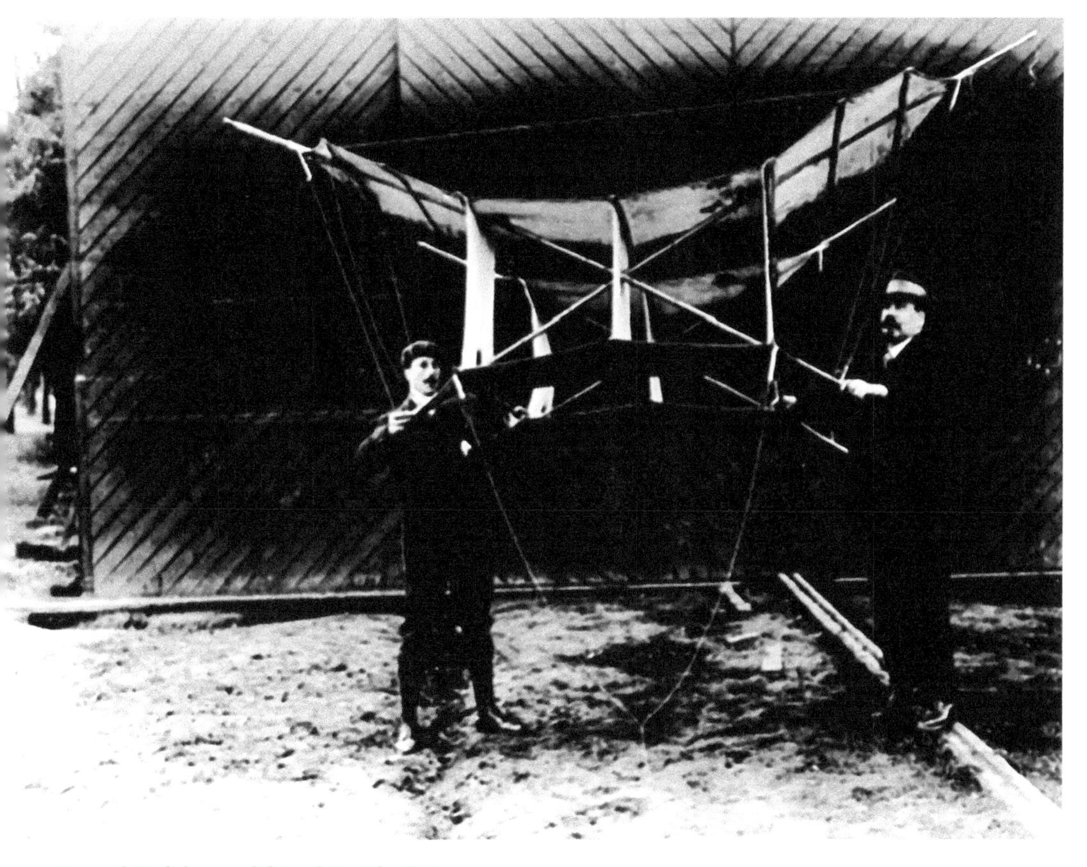

Samuel Cody's man-lifting kite, The Bat.

Later in 1909, aviation pioneers Horace, Eustace and Oswald Short of Short Brothers plc set up the world's first commercial aeroplane factory at Shellbeach, Isle of Sheppey. The first machines produced at their factory were for American aviation pioneers Wilber and Orville Wright, who visited several times. On 30 October 1909, John Theodore Cuthbert Moore-Brabazon made the first controlled flight by a British pilot over British soil. He flew a circular mile at Eastchurch Airfield in a Short Biplane No. 2, earning Eastchurch the title, 'Home of British Aviation'.

The opportunities to weaponize aeroplanes had not escaped the War Office and Admiralty and in 1910 they relocated the factory to Eastchurch, Isle of Sheppey, where they set up a base for naval aviator training and aircraft development and created the world's first tailless twin-engine aircraft. In 1912 they began designing, constructing and producing seaplanes capable of destroying the biggest airships of the day. The year 1912 also saw the formation of the Royal Flying Corps (RFC) as the new aviation wing of the army, and the Royal Naval Air Service (RNAS) as the new aviation wing of the navy. In 1918, both wings amalgamated to form the world's first independent air force, the Royal Air Force.

Building upon their seaplane's success, in 1913 the Short brothers moved from Eastchurch to expand their business, purchasing 8 acres of land with access to the sea at Rochester.

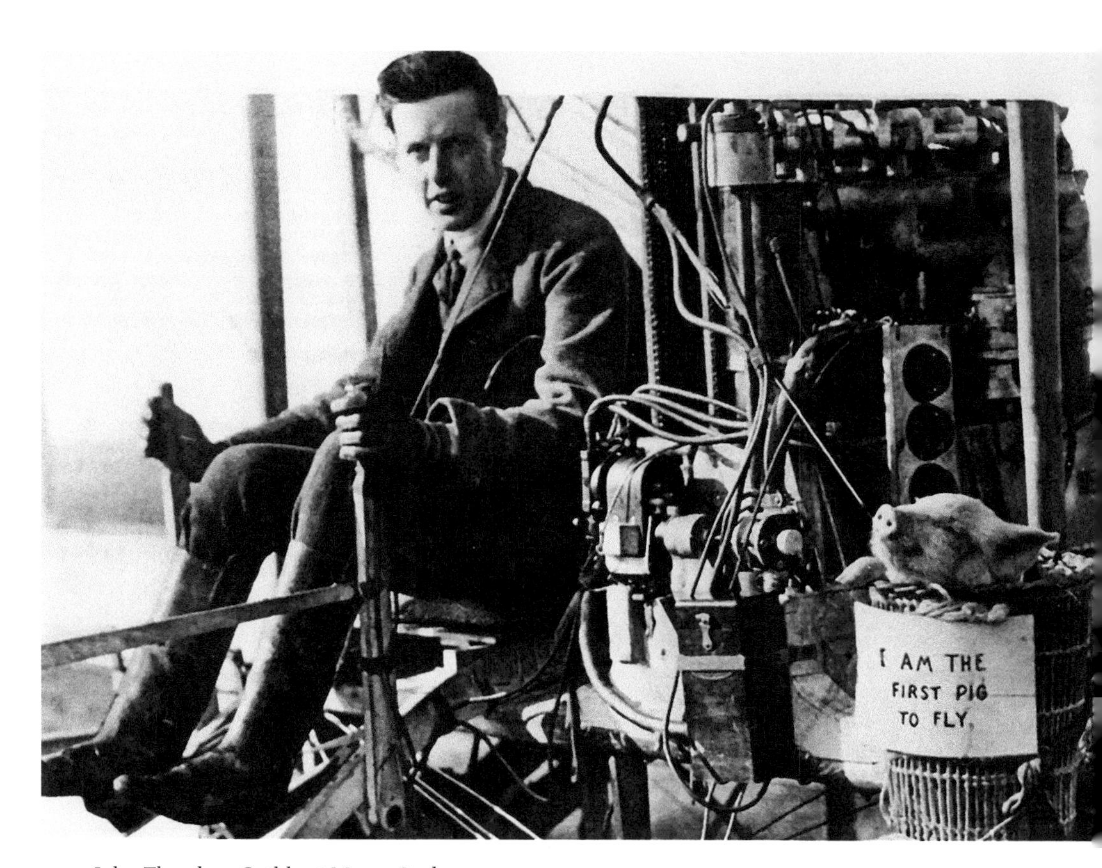

John Theodore Cuthbert Moore-Brabazon.

SHORT BROS.
Aeroplane & Balloon
- - Manufacturers, - -
LONDON & SHEPPEY.

Sole Manufacturers and Agents
in Great Britain & Ireland for
Messrs. Wilbur & Orville Wright.

EARLY DELIVERIES for
WRIGHT MACHINES can be
given, fitted with both wheels & skids.

BALLOON WORKS:
Battersea & Clapham,
LONDON.
Telegrams—"Ballooning, London."
Telephone—788 Battersea.

AEROPLANE WORKS:
Eastchurch & Shellbeach,
SHEPPEY.
Telegrams—"Flight, Eastchurch."
Telephone—5B Minster-on-Sea.

Short Brothers advertising poster. (AA)

The RNAS took over the Short Brothers site at Eastchurch, establishing their headquarters and a flying school there. Among their many achievements there, the RNAS conducted Britain's first bomb-dropping experiments and the first machine-gun-firing during flight. In 1950 Eastchurch was redeveloped and is now home to three prisons: HMP Elmley, Standford Hill and Swaleside. Today a few of the original aircraft hangars can be seen.

Following the outbreak of war in 1914, Short Brothers won the contract to supply the RNAS with their 'Short Admiralty Type 184' seaplane. The reliable two-seater, folding-wing, reconnaissance, bomb- and torpedo-carrying machine became the first aircraft to sink a ship by torpedo during the Battle of Gallipoli in 1917. The RNAS stationed at St Mildred's Bay used Short Brothers seaplanes to patrol the Channel and Thames Estuary in search of U-boats between 1914 and 1918. The Short brothers' association with Rochester and the military continued into the Second World War when they created the iconic Sunderland Flying Boat, but in 1948 they moved their operations to Belfast. Today, other than the slipway, nothing above ground exists of their factory at Rochester. However, underground tunnels constructed for additional factory space behind the Esplanade remain intact.

Commissioned in 1913, the Seaplane Base on the Hoo Peninsula, Isle of Grain, was one of the earliest naval air stations in Kent. By 1915 the base had become home to 'The Experimental Armament Section' and the 'Seaplane Test Flight and Experimental Construction Section'. Amalgamated in 1918, they became the Marine Experimental

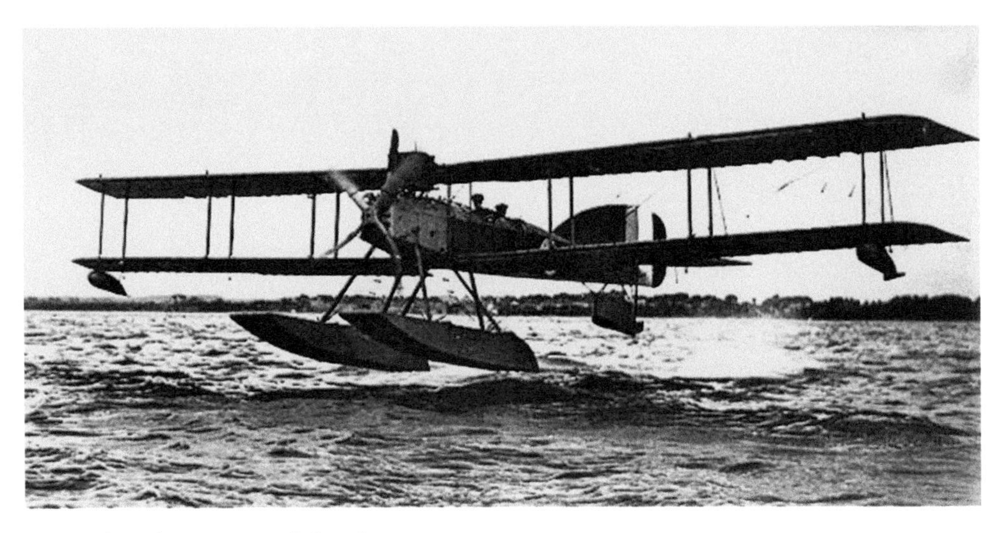

Short Admiralty 184 - torpedo-bomber.

Aircraft Depot. The depot developed flotation systems, armaments and undertook the first trials of aircraft to ship's deck-landings. In 1914, the navy constructed RNAS Kingsnorth as a training school for airship captains and technical staff. Throughout the war they used it as a base for anti-submarine patrols in the Thames Estuary and English Channel. The site is now a commercial retail park; the only remains to be seen are one of the original buildings and an airship shed, moved to nearby Moat Farm, St Mary Hoo. Another air station was established in 1915 at Capel-le-Ferne, Folkestone, which is now a caravan park. Only one earthwork and part of a hangar floor remains of the site.

During the First World War, the RFC built airfields at Bekesbourne, Biggin Hill and Dartford as part of the wider London Air Defence Area. As well as their defensive roles, Biggin Hill conducted wireless experiments, and Dartford undertook pilot training. The No. 2 Wireless School was located at Penshurst and West Malling, Throwley, Lympne, and Marden were designated emergency landing grounds. Later, following the commencement of hostilities in 1939, many RAF stations were upgraded and converted to operational airfields under the control of Eleven Group Fighter Command. Biggin Hill, Detling, Eastchurch, Gravesend, Hawkinge, Lympne, Manston and West Malling all saw active service during the Battle of Britain.

Much of the tangible heritage of these locations has disappeared with the passage of time, yet their symbolic and spiritual attraction are beacons for pilgrimage. The new Biggin Hill Memorial Museum tells the story of Britain's most famous fighter station, retaining some buildings of the period. In the grounds is a Heritage Hangar that houses the greatest concentration of Spitfires anywhere in the world. RAF Eastchurch, now an aviation museum, tells the history of the location and displays many associated exhibits. The former RAF Hawkinge is the oldest museum in the country dedicated to the Battle of Britain. At RAF Lympne derelict buildings and defensive structures survive, while RAF Gravesend is now a golf course, and at RAF Manston along with the museum some of the original station buildings remain.

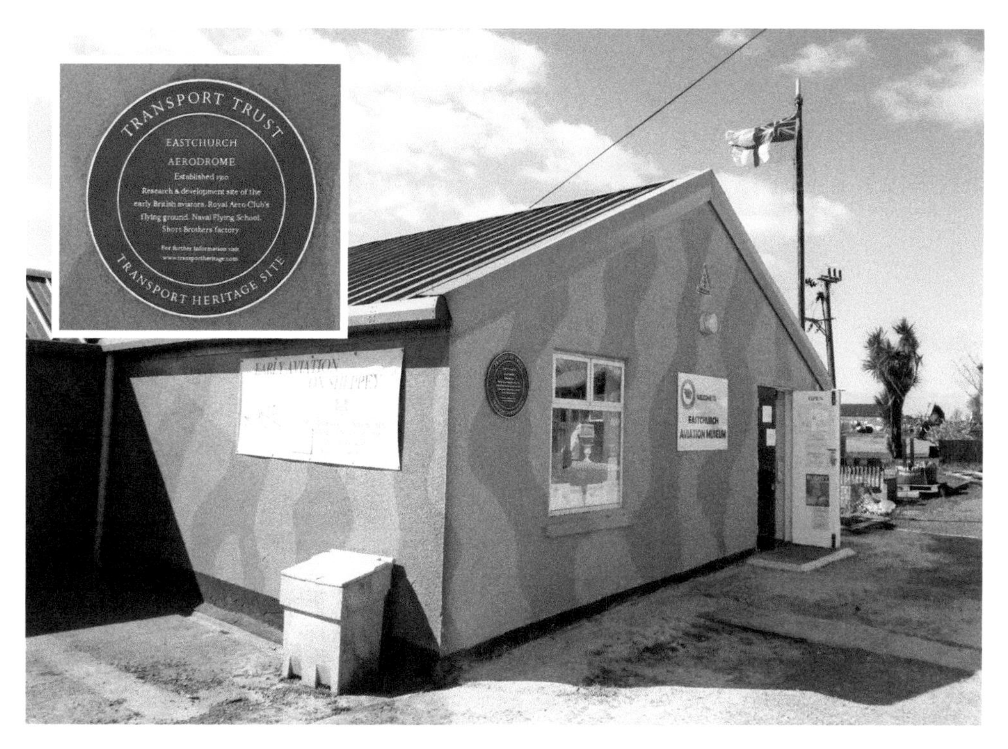

Eastchurch Aviation Museum.

Inset: Plaque, Eastchurch Aviation Museum.

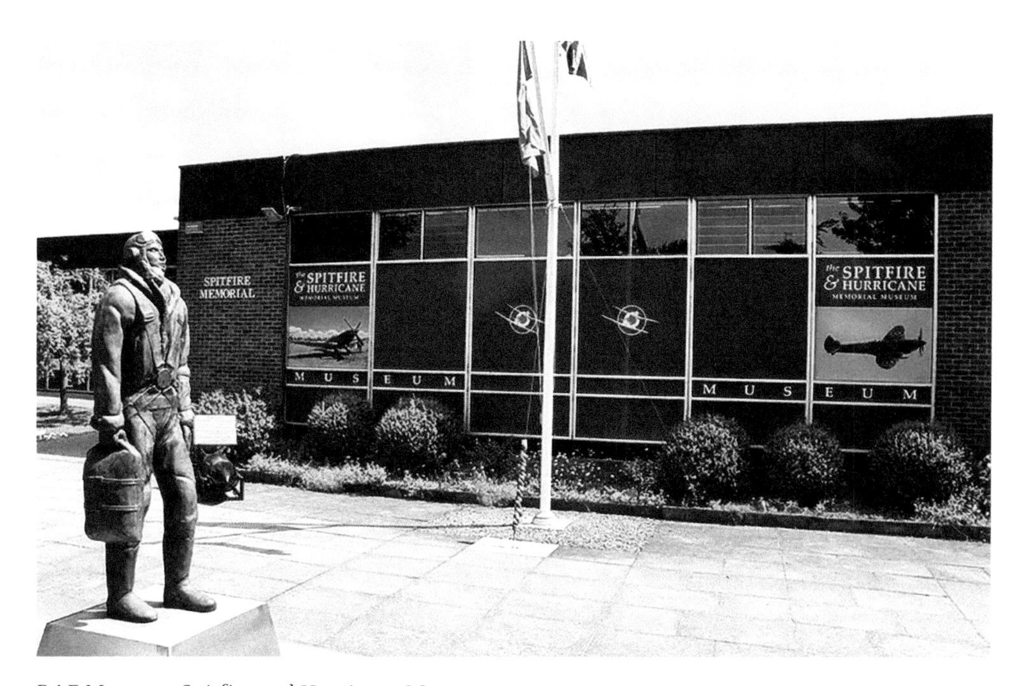

RAF Manston, Spitfire and Hurricane Museum.

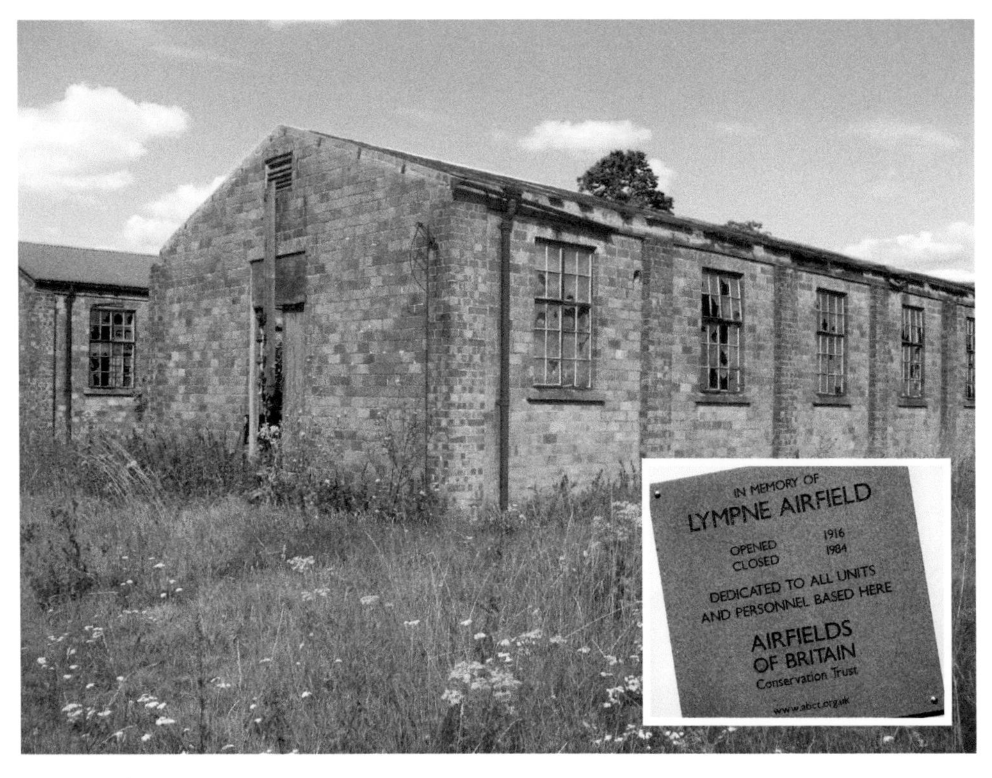

Remains of RAF Lympne.

Inset: Plaque, RAF Lympne.

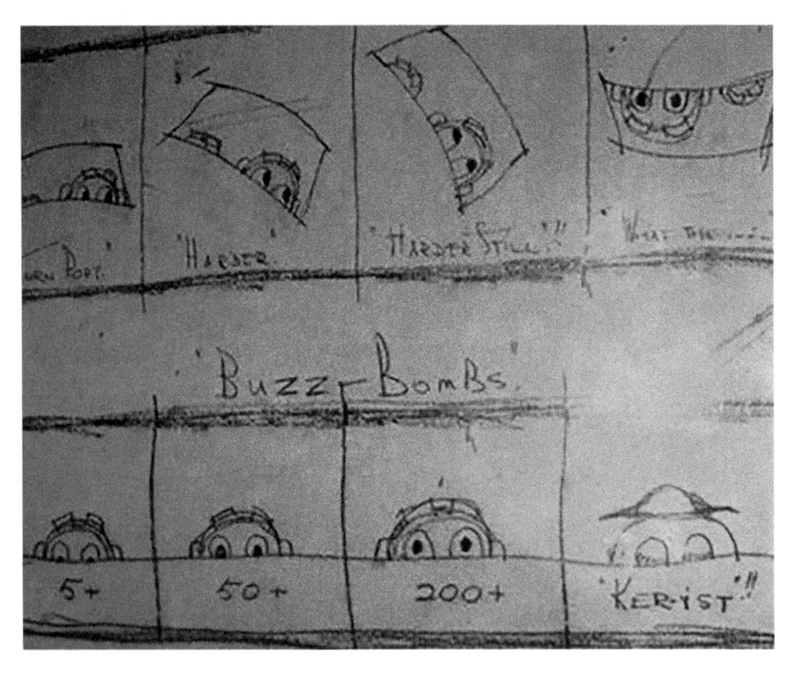

Cartoons at the Twitch Inn.

The Second Wolrd War headquarters and mess for officers flying from RAF West Malling was Douces Manor. Although the airfield is now Kings Hill housing development, the manor's cellar bar remains the only link to one of Britain's most epic periods in history. Accessible to the public on specific days during the year, the bar was known by the fighter pilots as 'Twitch Inn' because of the nervous afflictions displayed by many aviators dealing with the immense stress, strain and fatigue of aerial combat. Inside the bar, cartoons, graffiti carved into the walls and ceiling, and signatures written in candle smoke show their camaraderie and humour. The bar houses a permanent exhibition about the airfield during the Second World War.

Aviators and Air Personnel

Among the many pilots who have shaped the history of Kent's aviation, the McCudden brothers are Kent's most illustrious aviation family. The four brothers – James Thomas, John Anthony, William Henry, and Maurice Vincent – were of military stock. Their father, William, was a sergeant major in the Royal Engineers, whose father and grandfather had also served in the army. Their mother's father and grandfather served as naval Royal Marines.

Known as 'Barrack Rats', the nickname given to children born in Brompton Barracks' Garrison Hospital, Gillingham, the brothers joined the RFC during the First World War. Having first joined the Royal Engineers in 1910, James transferred to the Royal Flying Corps in 1913 as an air mechanic. By his death in 1918, aged twenty-two, he had risen to the rank of Temporary Major and become a flying ace with fifty-seven aerial victories, placing him seventh on the list of the First World War's most successful aces. The most highly decorated British pilot of the war, he held the VC, Distinguished Service Order and Bar, Military Cross and Bar, and Military Medal. He was also one of the longest-serving pilots. He died at Auxi-le-Château, France, on 9 July 1918 when his plane crashed following a routine take-off.

His brother John, a second lieutenant aged twenty and holder of the Military Cross, was also an ace. He died in combat over Busigny, near Le Cateau, France, on 18 March 1918. William, a flight sergeant (pilot instructor) with the Royal Flying Corps, had taught John and James to fly and died in an accident at Gosport, Hampshire, in June 1915, aged twenty-four. Maurice, too young for the war, worked as a flight test engineer but died from colonitis in 1931.

In February 1940 Commodore Gerald d'Erlanger formed the Air Transport Auxiliary (ATA) to release fighter pilots for combat duty. Responsible for transporting military aircraft from factories to maintenance units and ferrying men and planes around the UK, it employed capable women and male pilots not eligible for operational service. One such woman was Pauline Gower, born in Tonbridge, Kent, in 1910, who became an acclaimed aviator and flying instructor with 2,000 hours' flying experience. Gower was asked to organise the women's section of the ATA, nicknamed 'Attagirls'. Gower started flying at age eighteen and obtained her pilot's licence aged twenty in 1930 after just fifteen hours' flying time. The following year, she became the third woman in the world to earn a commercial pilot's licence. Gower and fellow aviator Dorothy Spicer started the first all-female air taxi and joy ride service operating from a field in Kent. She also performed at air shows up and down the country making a name for herself in aviation circles.

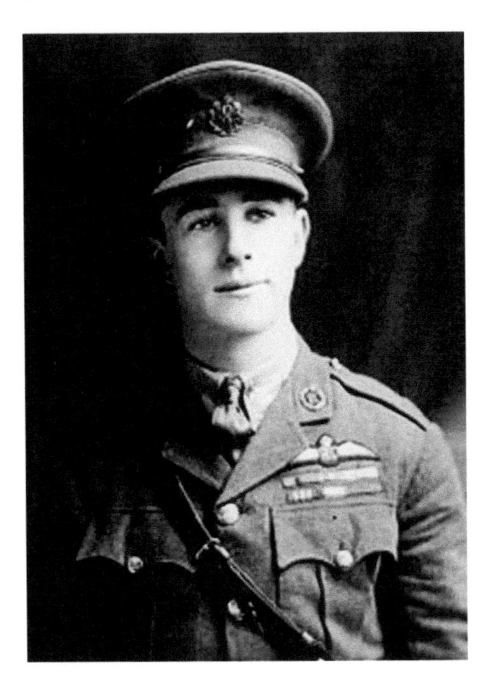

James McCudden.

When Gower became commandant of the women's section, there were nine female pilots in the ATA. Under her leadership and guidance, that number rose to over 150 women, flying many kinds of aeroplanes, from trainers to bombers. After the war she was awarded an MBE and became the first woman in the world to be appointed to the board of a civilian airline, as director of the British Overseas Airways Corporation.

Of the ATA's 166 female pilots, fifteen lost their lives in the air, including legendary pioneer aviator Amy Johnson CBE. Born 1 July 1903, she was the first woman in the UK to become a licensed aviation ground engineer and qualified as a pilot in 1929. She achieved worldwide recognition in 1930, becoming the first woman pilot to fly solo from England to Australia and set many records. In 1931 Johnson became the first pilot to fly from London to Moscow in one day and in 1932 she flew solo from London to Cape Town, South Africa, breaking her husband's earlier record by over eleven hours.

Johnson joined the ATA in 1940, and on 5 January 1941 she was tasked with delivering a twin-engine monoplane to RAF Kidlington, Oxford. Having left Blackpool, bad weather caused her to fly off course. Her plane was seen off Herne Bay around 15.30 hrs and a short time later she was observed parachuting through the snow. A recovery boat reached her but due to rough seas rescue attempts failed. She disappeared when the current from the boat's propeller dragged her and her travelling bag underwater. Parts of her plane and some of her possessions were washed ashore, but Johnson's body was never recovered.

Many pilots gained distinction and notoriety while flying from airfields in Kent. Among them are Wing Commander Guy Gibson, VC, DSO & Bar, DFC & Bar, leader of the Dam Buster raids and a member of the Tovil Venture Scouts, based at West Malling. Wing

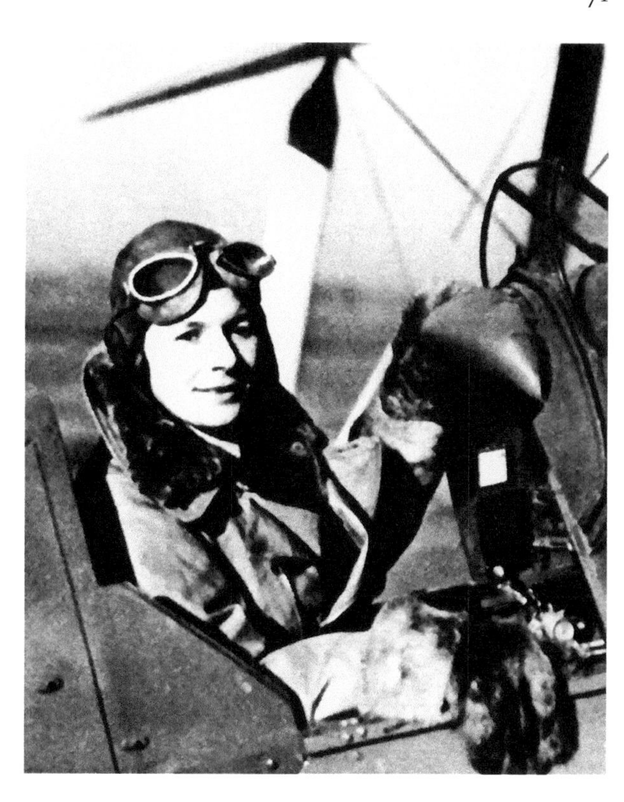

Pauline Gower.

Commander Adolph Malan, DSO & Bar, DSC & Bar, creator of 'rules for fighter-pilots', was stationed at Biggin Hill, while the most successful night-time fighter crew, Wing Commander 'Cats Eyes' Cunningham, CBE, DSO & Two Bars, DFC & Bar, and his air gunner, Pilot Officer Cecil 'Jimmy' Rawnsley DSO, DFC, DFM & Bar, along with Kent's own Roderick Learoyd, were all based at West Malling.

Not all RAF acts of bravery took place in the cockpits and fuselages. Some happened in the heat of battle on the ground, on airfields and in airbases. The actions of three individuals merit mention. Sergeant Joan Mortimer, Flight Officer Elspeth Henderson and Sergeant Helen Turner of the Women's Auxiliary Air Force (WAAF) were awarded the Military Medal (MM) for their bravery. While stationed at RAF Biggin Hill during the Battle of Britain, all three remained at their posts throughout a series of Luftwaffe raids on 1 September 1940. Henderson kept in contact with Fighter Command Headquarters, Uxbridge, despite the operations room where she was working being hit by a bomb that knocked her to the ground. Turner was in another part of the building and kept the switchboard operational until a fire broke out; both women gave up their posts only when commanded. Mortimer was in the armoury surrounded by several tons of high explosive when the air raid started. She also operated a telephone switchboard relaying messages to the defence posts around the airfield. When the surprise attack finished, Mortimer hurried onto the airfield with red flags and marked the locations of unexploded bombs strewn around the area. One detonated, knocking her over, but she carried on.

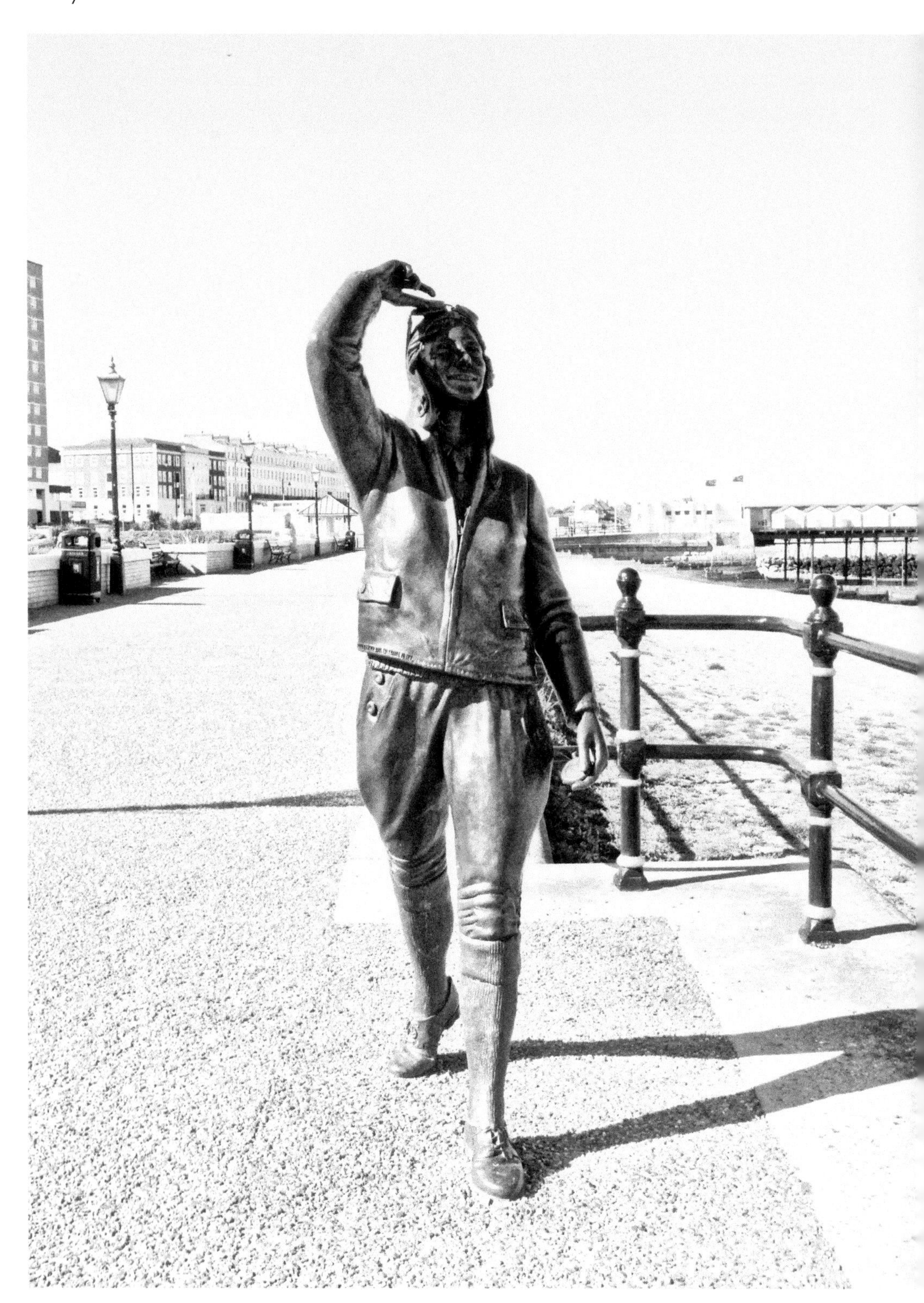

Amy Johnson, Herne Bay.

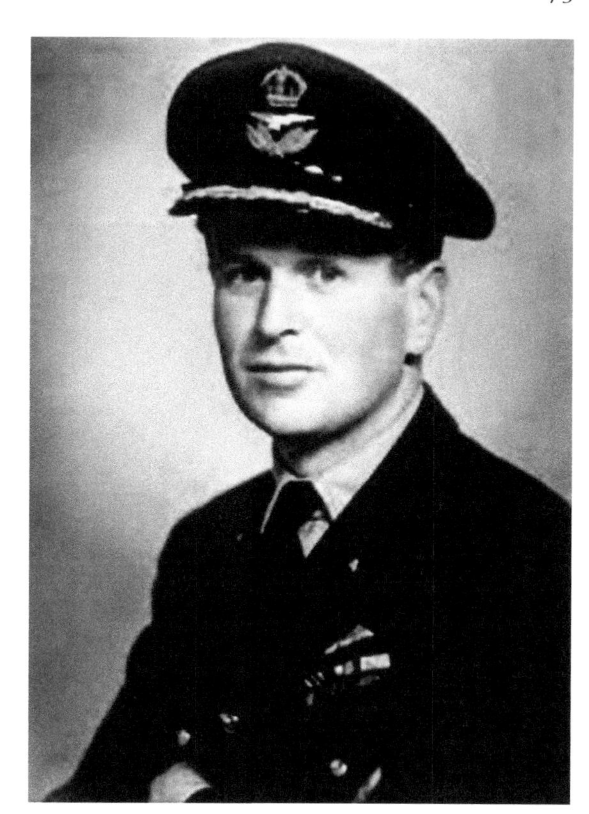

Right: Wing Commander 'Cats Eyes' Cunningham.

Below: Sergeant Joan Mortimer, Flight Officer Elspeth Henderson and Sergeant Helen Turner.

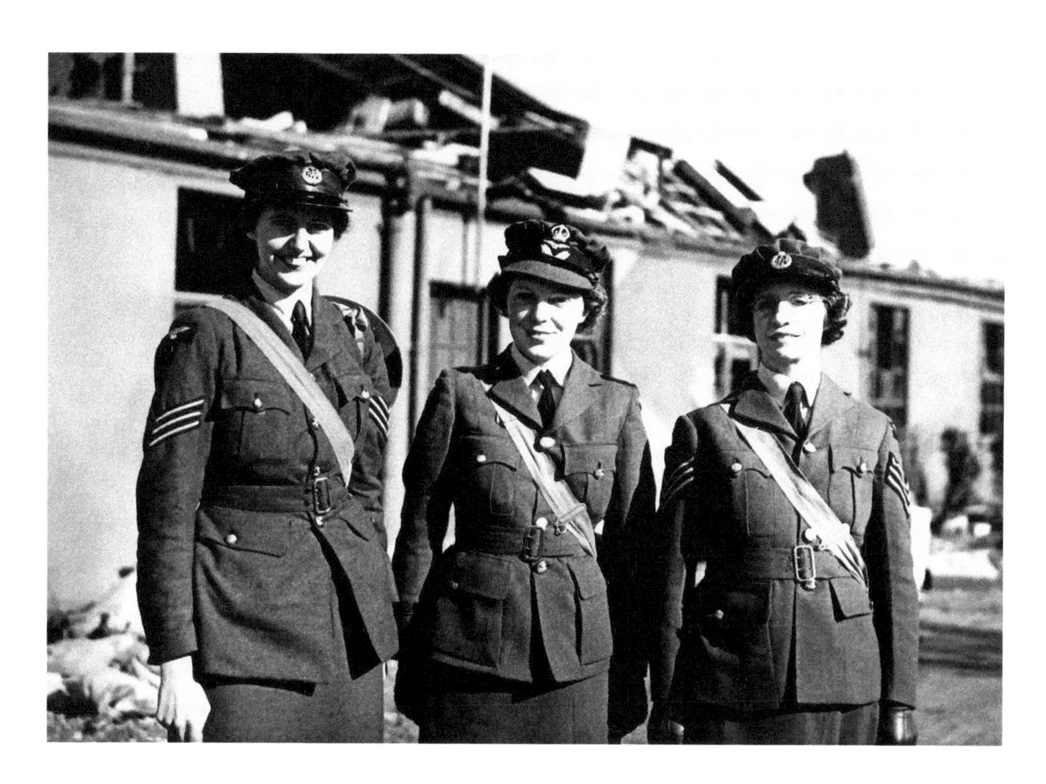

During the war years, Kent was home to many remarkable individuals whose unique talents contributed to the war effort. One such scientist, engineer and inventor was Sir Barnes Wallis. A former sub-lieutenant in the RNAS, Wallis invented the 'Bouncing Bomb' during the Second World War. This was an innovative and groundbreaking piece of engineering that enabled a previously unattackable target to be bombed. Following extensive trials off the coast of Herne Bay and Thanet, the bombs were successfully deployed in Germany in 1943 by 617 squadron the 'Dam Busters', led by Wing Commander Guy Gibson during Operation Chastise, during which the Sorpe Dam was damaged and the Möhne and Eder dams destroyed.

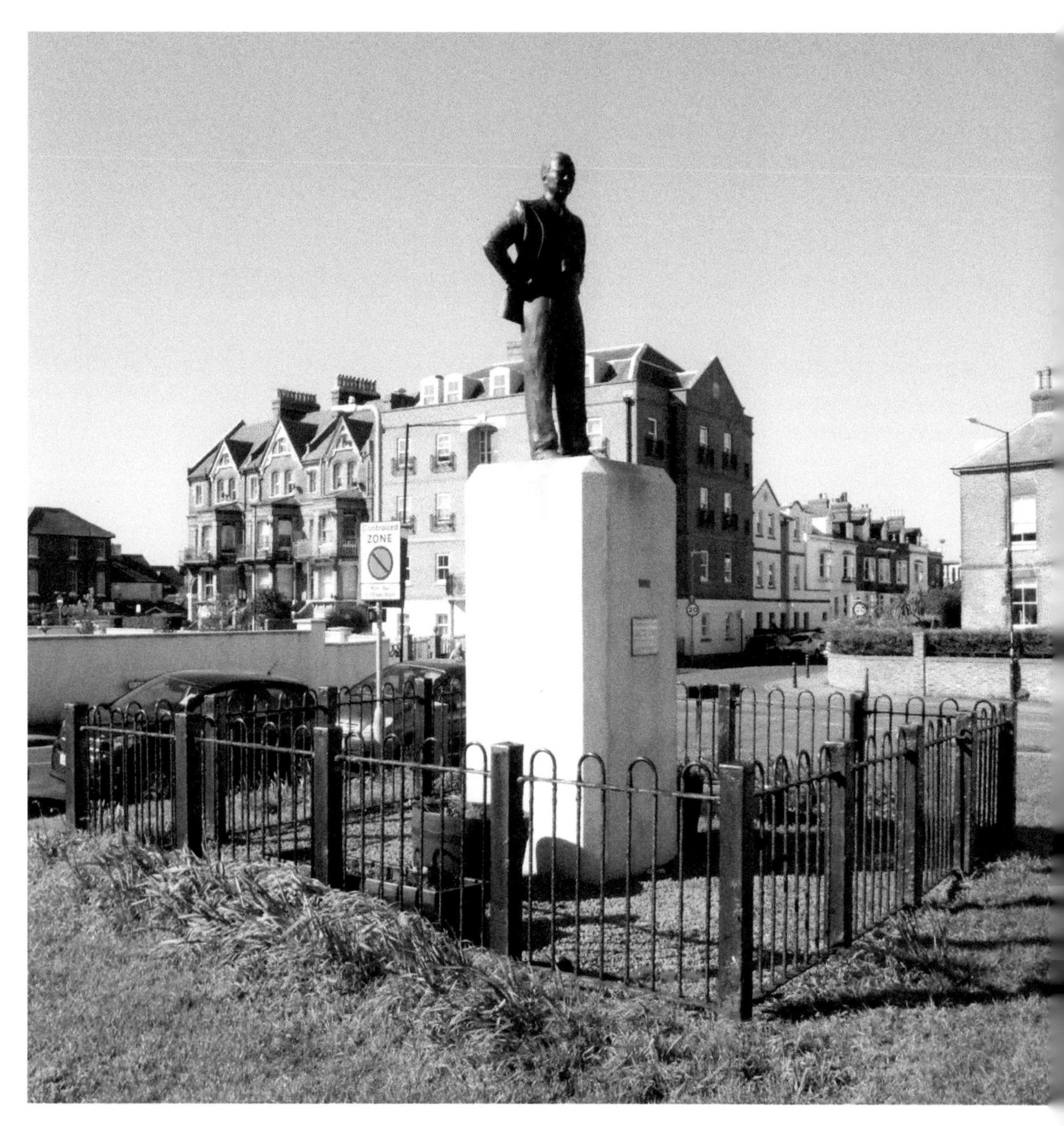

Barnes Wallis, Herne Bay.

7. Devils, Royals and Old Buffs

Before the English Civil War, the army was drawn from local militia formed by district officials or private forces mobilised piecemeal by nobility. The regimental system we know today has its foundations in the seventeenth century. Aristocrats and professional soldiers were commissioned at the rank of colonel and expected to raise, dress and equip their own regiments. Later reforms aligned these regiments with geographic areas such as counties. Kent had two regiments: the Queen's Own Regiment and the East Kent Regiment of Foot. Both have a long and distinguished military history forged by the deeds, achievements and sacrifices of generations of local men and women. Today their heritage exists thanks to the determination and dedication of people who protect, preserve and champion that heritage.

The 52nd Queen's Own Regiment was founded in 1756. Two years later, it was assigned the added title '50th Foot'. In 1782, keeping its numerical regimental classification, it adopted the regional title the West Kent Regiment. In 1831 the regiment became the Queen's Own Regiment of Foot. After further reforms in 1881, it amalgamated with the 97th (Earl of Ulster's) Regiment of Foot to create four battalions of the Queen's Own Royal West Kent Regiment, comprising around 3,000 men. The regiment's name underwent further changes: in 1920 it became the Royal West Kent Regiment (Queen's Own); in 1961 the Queen's Own Buffs, the Royal Kent Regiment; in 1966 the Queen's Regiment; and in 1992, the Princess of Wales's Royal Regiment.

The regimental mottos 'Invictus' (unconquered) and 'Quo Fas et Gloria Ducunt' (whither right and glory lead) define the regiment's character, and during its existence it has held several nicknames. Following the Egyptian campaign of 1801, a large percentage of the regiment suffered from ophthalmia, an eye disease that caused long- and short-term visual impairment. As a result, they became known as 'The Blind Half Hundred'. Later during the Peninsular War, they were called 'The Dirty Half-Hundred' because the dye from the black cuffs on their tunics made their skin turn black when they wiped their sweat away. They were also known as 'The Devil's Royals' following their celebrated charge and rout of five French regiments at the Battle of Vimeiro in 1808.

Throughout their worldwide service they fought with distinction, receiving eighteen battle honours. Their campaigns included the French Revolutionary Wars (1792–1802), the Peninsular War (1808–14), the Gwalior Campaign (1843), the First Sikh War (1845-46), the Crimean War (1854–56) and the Second Maori War (1863–66). During the First World War, the regiment was awarded sixty-five battle honours across three war zones and added another forty-one battle honours during the Second World War. Further name changes followed. In 1920 they became the Royal West Kent Regiment (Queen's Own) and in 1961, the Queen's Own Buffs, the Royal Kent Regiment. In 1966 they were merged

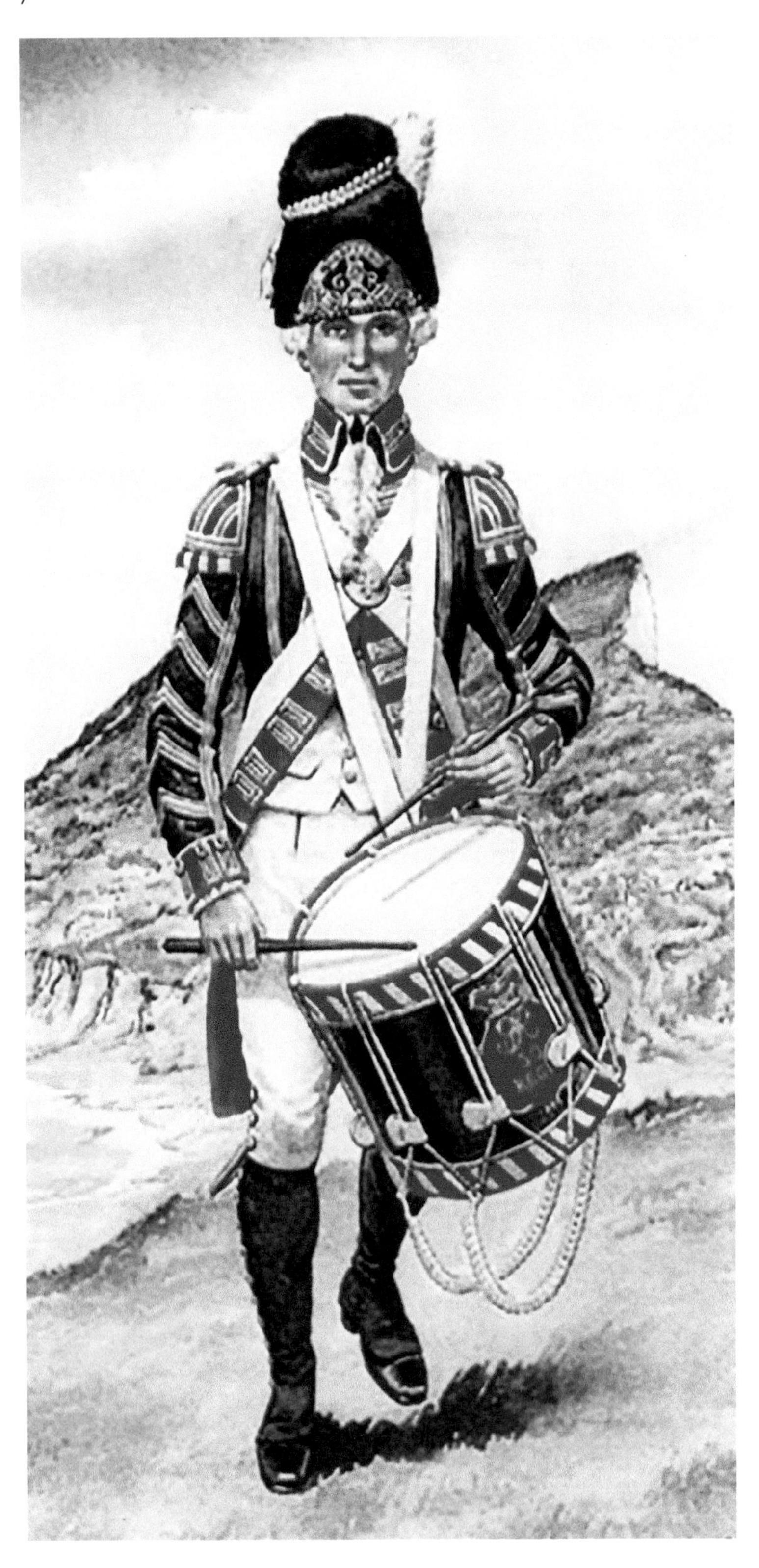

Drummer of the 50th foot *c.* 1755.

to form the Queen's Regiment and following the latest restructure in 1992 they were amalgamated with the Hampshire Regiment to become 'The Princess of Wales's Royal Regiment' (PWRR).

The regiment boasts six VCs and the first Dickens Medal issued for gallantry to a dog. Bob, a large white collie-Labrador cross served with the 6th Battalion from Dunkirk to Italy. He received his award for preventing the capture and saving the lives of his patrol on 24 March 1944 in North Africa. However, in 1946 in Italy, while with his handler, he slipped his leash. Despite desperate press releases seeking his return, he was not seen again. At the Queen's Own Royal West Kent Regimental Museum in Maidstone is a life-size replica of Bob with his medal, and the medals of four of the VC winners.

Originating in Tudor times, the East Kent Regiment was one of the oldest regiments in the British Army. Like the Queen's Own Regiment, it underwent many reviews and name changes. Between 1572 and 1648 it was the Thomas Morgan's Company of Foot, in 1665 the 4th, the Holland Maritime Regiment, then the 4th, the Holland Regiment and from 1668 it became the 4th, the Lord High Admiral's Regiment. In 1737, as the new practice was to name regiments after their commanding colonel, it became the 3rd Howard's Regiment of Foot.

In 1744 the Honourable Sir Charles Howard commanded the regiment and Lieutenant General Thomas Howard commanded the 19th Regiment of Foot. Honouring tradition,

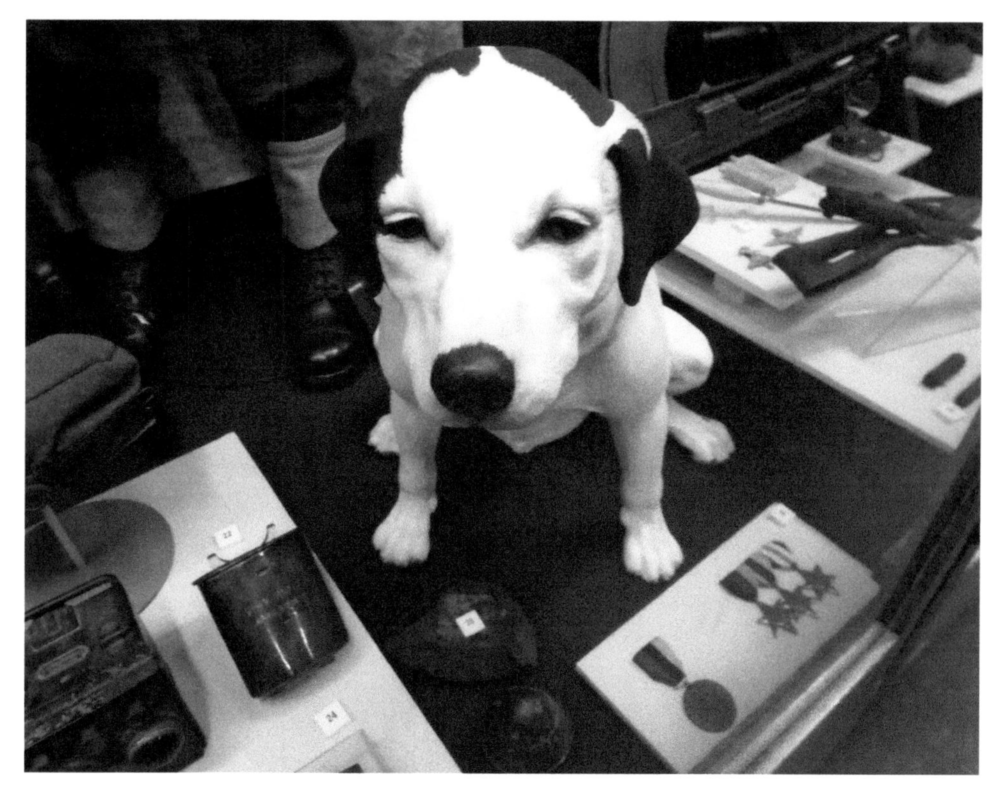

Bob and his medals.

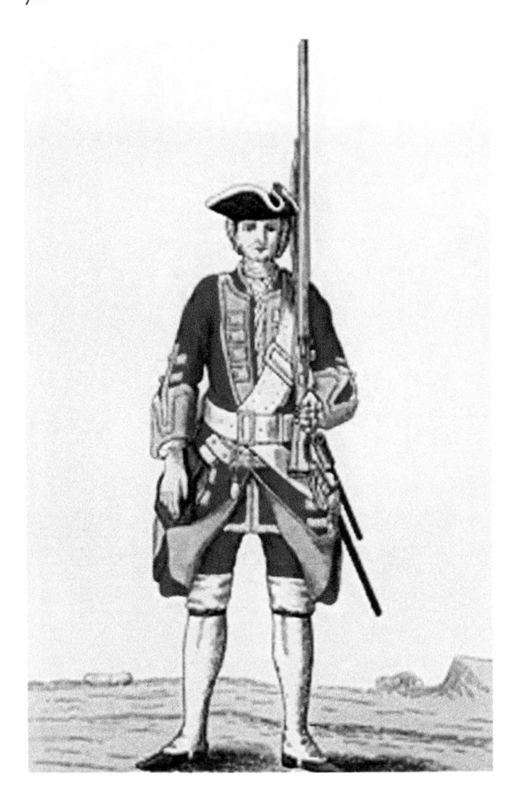

East Kent Regiment *c.* 1742.

both regiments were named after their colonels, becoming the Howard Regiments of Foot. To avoid confusion, the regiments took the colours of their facings (the colours added to uniforms to identify them) as part of their names. The 19th Foot became the Green Howards and the 3rd Foot became Howard's Buffs. In 1881 Howard's Buffs became the 3rd East Kent Regiment of Foot (The Buffs) until 1935 when they became known as The Buffs (East Kent Regiment).

The Buffs' motto, 'Veteri Frondescit Honore' (Its Ancient Honour Flourishes), acknowledges their length of service and achievements. Like the West Kent's, the Buffs were a formidable fighting force with an outstanding combat record. Among their achievements, they received 116 Battle Honours from engagements fought during many conflicts including the Napoleonic Wars (1803–15), the Crimean War (1853–56), the Zulu War (1879) and both World Wars. During the latter conflicts, four soldiers were awarded the Victoria Cross, among them William Richard Cotter, born in Folkestone, Kent, in 1882. In 1916 Cotter was a thirty-three-year-old Acting Corporal in the 6th Battalion, East Kent Regiment, when he was awarded the Victoria Cross for his bravery near Hohenzollern Redoubt, France.

On 6 March his leg was blown off at the knee and he was also wounded in both arms. Despite this, he made his way unaided for 50 yards to a crater, steadied the men who were holding it, controlled their fire, issued orders and encouraged them to stand fast when counter-attacks were launched at them. For two hours he held his position, only allowing his wounds to be roughly dressed when the attacks had quietened down. Because of enemy fire he and his men were unable to leave the crater and remained there for fourteen

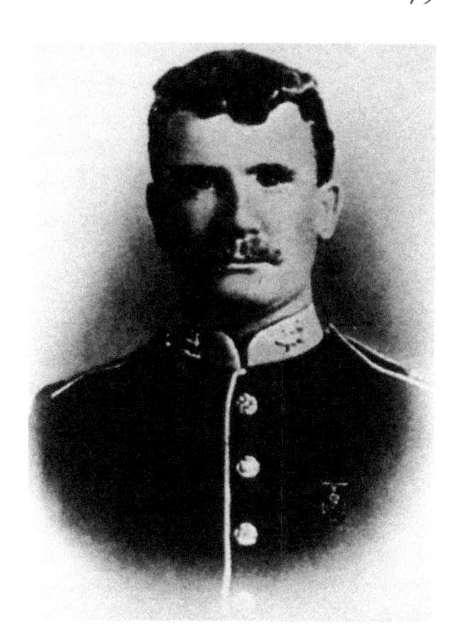

Corporal William Cotter VC.

hours, during which time it is said he had a cheery word for everyone. Following his rescue, he died from his wounds and was buried at Lillers Communal Cemetery, France.

Following a series of mergers and reforms from 1961 to 1992, the Buffs now form part of the history and heritage of the PWRR. Much of the history and heritage of the regiment can be viewed at the Buffs Regimental Museum, Canterbury.

In 1794, amidst fears of a French invasion, Kent formed two volunteer cavalry regiments: the Queen's Own West Kent Yeomanry and the Royal East Kent Yeomanry. Despite defending the county, through necessity both were used alongside regular units during the Second Boer War and the First World War, gaining many battle honours. In 1920, both yeomanry regiments were amalgamated as the 6th (Kent) Army Brigade, Royal Field Artillery.

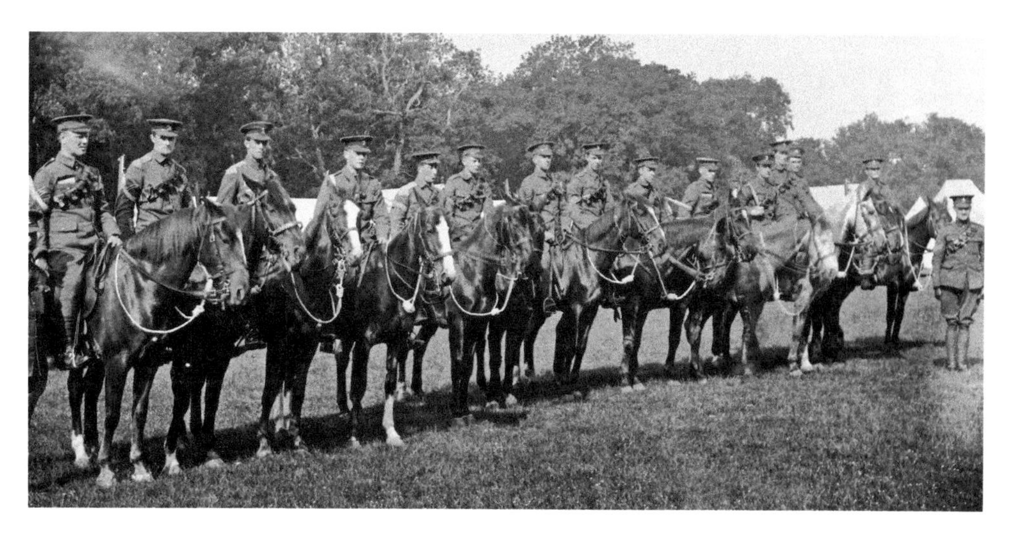

East Kent Yeomanry.

8. Cemeteries, Memorials and Monuments

The county's burial grounds, churchyards and military cemeteries are the resting place for several thousand Commonwealth War Graves Commission burials and many other important armed forces interments. Often unknown and overlooked, thousands of monuments and memorials to the people, places and events linked to the county's military heritage exist across the county.

Fort Pitt Military Cemetery, Rochester

Created before the Crimean War, this cemetery, found on the main A299 Chatham-Maidstone road, remains in use. Most of the burials are of Commonwealth War Graves, 256 from the First World War and twenty-three from the Second World War. The cemetery also includes the Commonwealth War Graves Commission Cross of Sacrifice as well as many interesting private monuments.

The entranceway is dominated by a large stone monument that is at the top of a short rise and accessed via a set of white gates decorated with ornate swords. The monument, mounted with a cannon, rifles, hammers and pickaxes, commemorates the lives of the

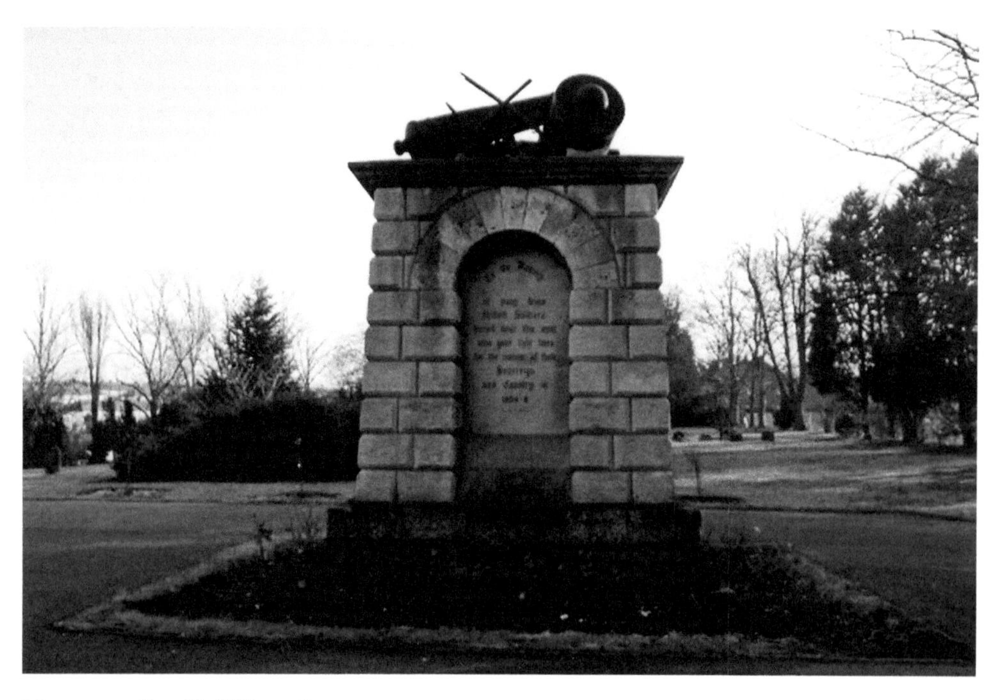

Monument, Fort Pit Military Cemetery.

men buried nearby. Many fought in the Crimean War, the Second Opium War (1856–60), the Anglo-Persian War (1856–57), and the Indian Mutiny (1857) and succumbed to their injuries at nearby Fort Pitt Military Hospital,

Shorncliffe Military Cemetery, Folkestone

Established around 1855, the cemetery is the resting place for soldiers from almost every regiment that has existed, along with wives, children and civilian workers. The first recorded interment was on 28 August 1856: Private George Burrows, 6th Inniskilling Dragoons, who died of wounds sustained during the Crimean War. It is uncertain where soldiers and those associated with nearby Shorncliffe camp were buried before this time, but it is generally accepted that they rest in unmarked graves within nearby Cheriton Churchyard.

Of the 497 First World War burials at the cemetery, 305 are Canadian. One is a member of the Portuguese Expeditionary Corps and six are members of the Chinese Labour Corps. There is also a memorial wall commemorating eighteen Belgian soldiers who were originally interred within a large mausoleum there. However, following a landslip, this was destroyed and later removed following the Second World War.

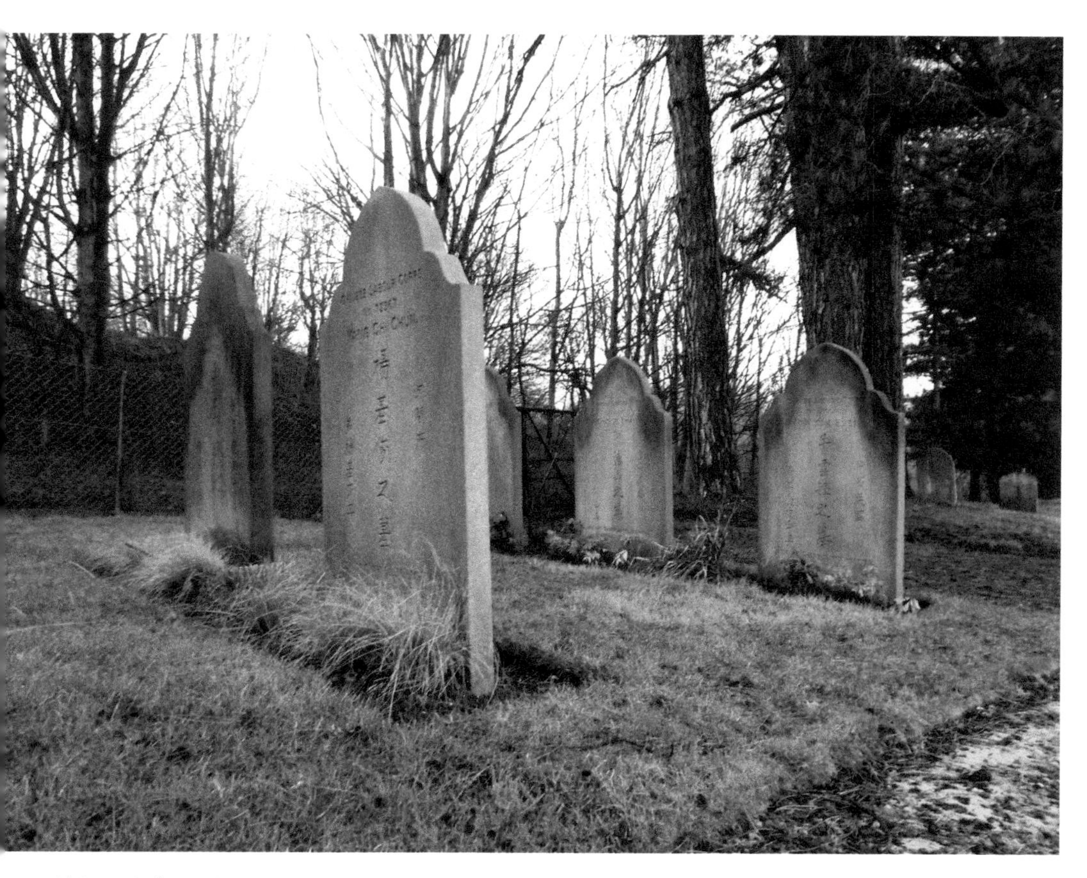

Chinese Labour Corps.

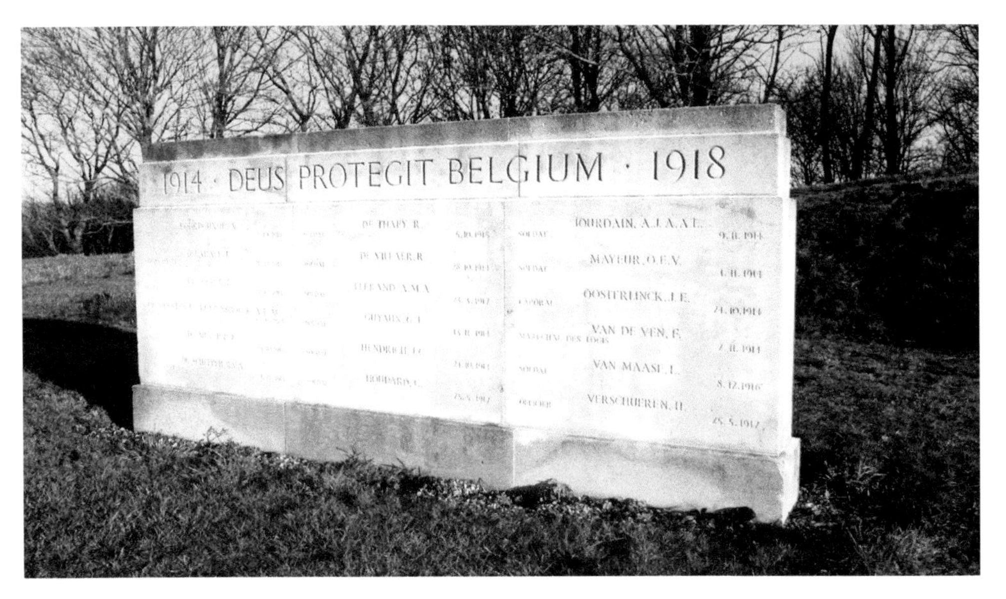

Commemorative wall to Belgian soldiers.

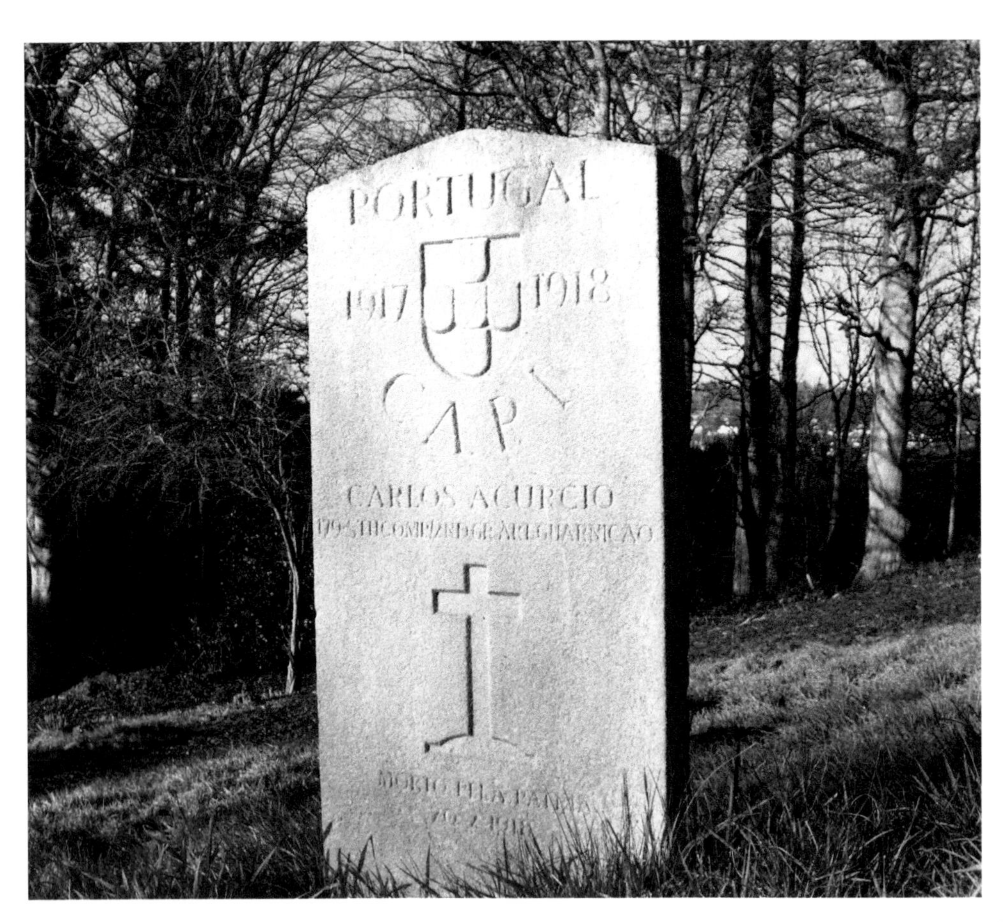

Portuguese Expeditionary Corps.

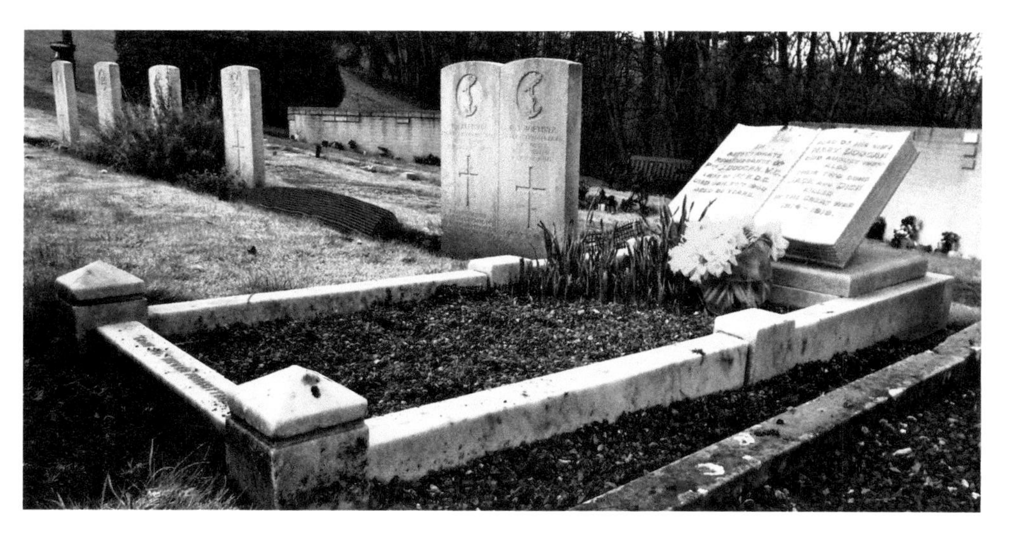

Grave of Private John Doogan VC.

Kent cemeteries hold the remains of twenty-nine Victoria Cross recipients and three of them rest within the grounds of Shorncliffe Military Cemetery:

Sergeant Joseph Charles Brennan, Royal Regiment Artillery (Indian Mutiny, 3 April 1858)
Private Patrick McHale, Royal Northumberland Fusiliers (Indian Mutiny, 2 October 1857)
Private John Doogan, Queens Dragoon Guards (1st Boer War 28 January 1881).

All Saints Military Cemetery, Orpington

Known locally as the 'Ontario Cemetery' and 'Canadian Corner', All Saints Military Cemetery is a purpose-built extension to the churchyard. It contains the burials of 146 First World War and Second World War casualties, including eighty-eight Canadian,

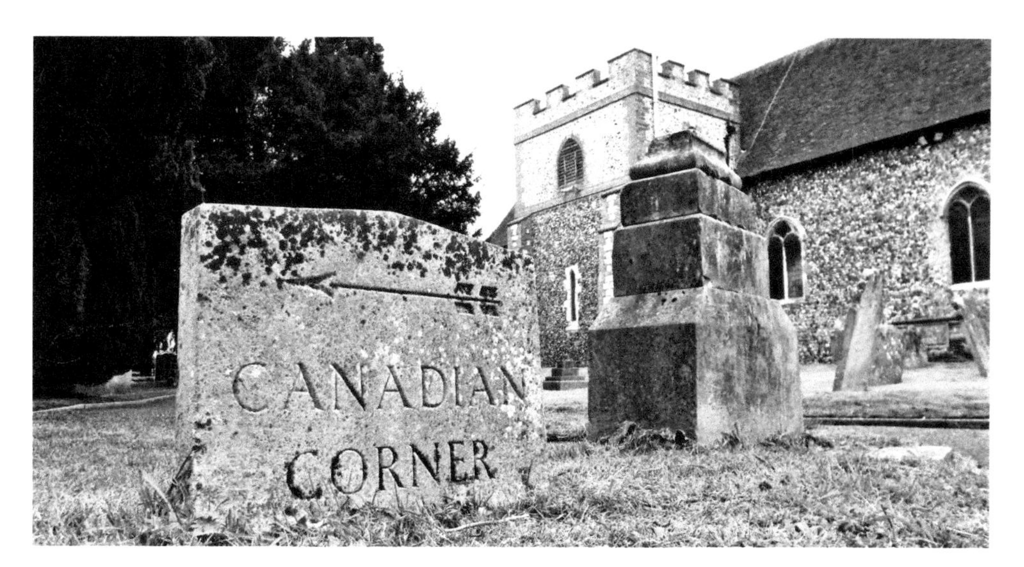

Canadian Cemetery, Orpington.

fifty-three British and five Australian service personnel; it also holds seventy non-war military graves. Most came from the nearby Ontario Hospital at Orpington, which was purpose-built and in use from February 1916 to September 1917, when it became No. 16 Canadian General Hospital. It closed in September 1919. The design of the cemetery is unique, resembling those found in France and Belgium. The Memorial Cross, unveiled in 1921 by the High Commissioner for Canada, was the first to be erected outside the Western Front and the first Canadian memorial unveiled in the UK.

Monuments

Kent's motto is 'Invicta', Latin for 'unconquered', and appears on the county council's coat of arms. Tradition states that it was adopted following the Norman invasion of 1066 when the people of Kent intercepted the Duke of Normandy en route to London. Their presence so scared William that he fled with his army, leaving Kent unconquered. Despite this he would become known as William the conqueror, something the people of Kent find quite amusing.

In the churchyard of St Peter and St Paul's in Swanscombe is a monument commemorating this event. The monument states:

> Near this spot by ancient tradition the men of Kent and Kentish men carrying boughs on their shoulders and swords in their hands met the invader William Duke of Normandy. They offered peace if he would grant their ancient rights and liberties otherwise war and that most deadly. Their request was granted and from that day the motto of Kent has been Invicta.

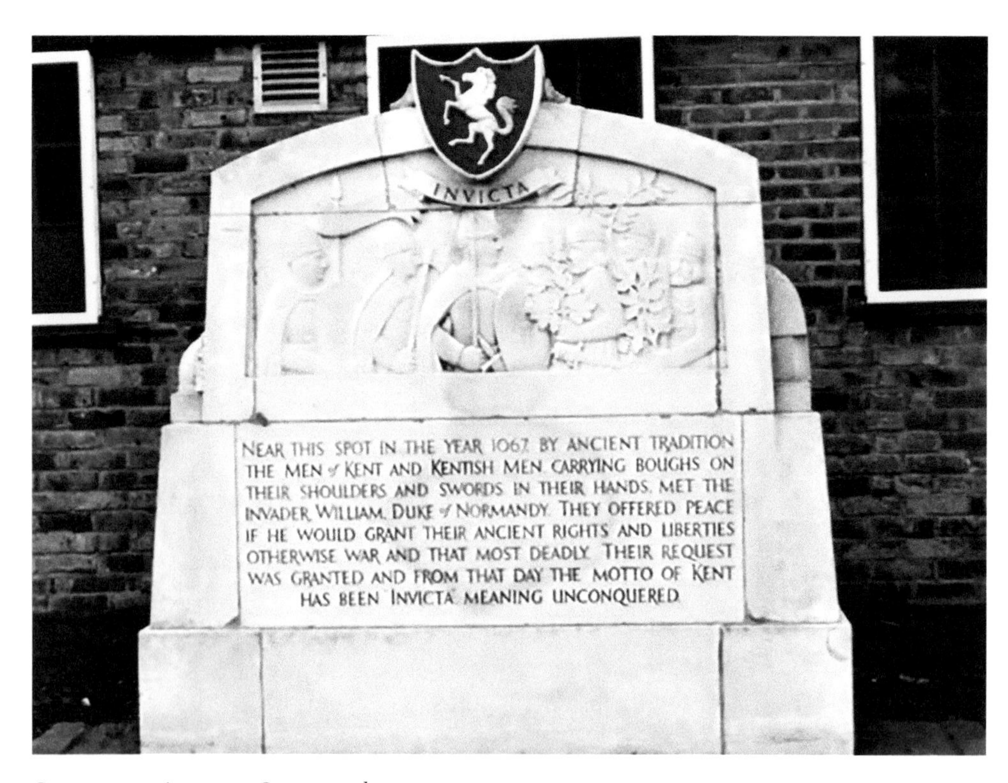

Commemorative stone, Swanscombe.

Of the many wonderful monuments to individuals, several stand out. A bronze statue of Squadron Leader Mohinder Pujji stands at Gravesend. This is an outstanding example of a monument to those who didn't have to fight for Britain but chose to. His statue commemorates all those from the Commonwealth who fought for Britain from the First World War to the present day. One of the first Sikh pilots to volunteer with the Royal Air Force, Pujji had one of the most amazing and enduring careers of any Second World War pilot. He had the rare distinction of operating twenty different aircraft in wars in Europe, North Africa, the Middle East and Asia. Arriving in the UK in 1940, he was stationed in Gravesend and fought in the Battle of Britain. During his career he lost a lung flying at high altitude, downed two aircraft and survived being shot down twice.

Pujji was awarded the Distinguished Flying Cross for actions while flying reconnaissance sorties over Japanese-occupied Burma. Flying through a monsoon, he displayed outstanding leadership and courage, gathering information that prevented 300 American soldiers from being attacked by Japanese troops. After the war Pujji returned to Gravesend where he lived until he died in 2010, aged ninety-two.

Admiral Sir Bertram Ramsay, mastermind and leader of the naval evacuation of Dunkirk in May 1940 and the naval assault on Normandy, France, in June 1944, is also remembered by a life-size statue at Dover Castle. The imposing figure of Field Marshal

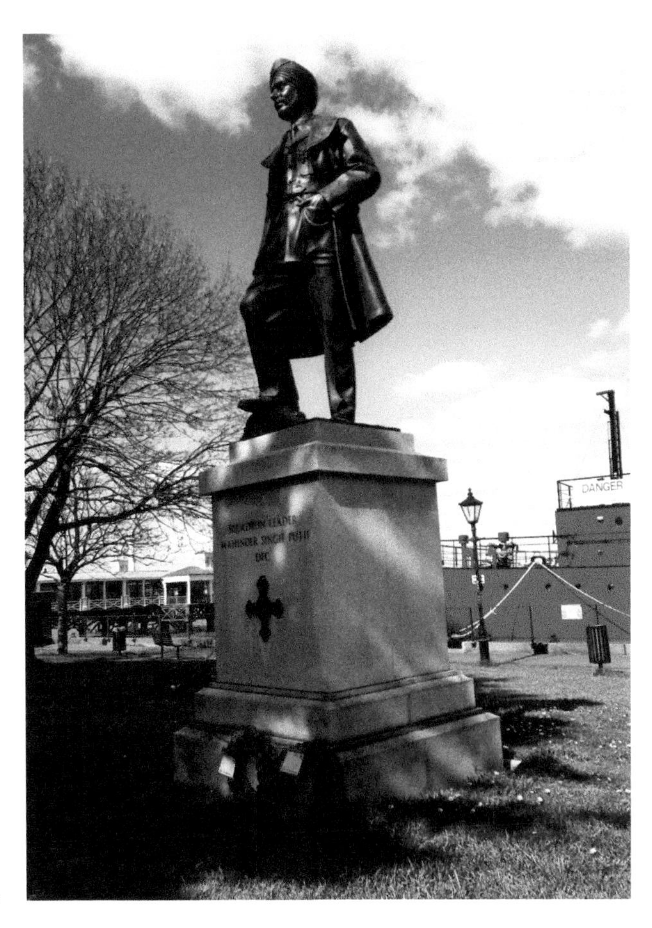

Squadron Leader Mohinder Pujji.

Horatio Herbert Kitchener (1850–1916), mounted on a horse, is in front of the former home of the School of Royal Engineers at Kitchener Barracks, Chatham (now a housing development). Commissioned into the Royal Engineers, he became their colonel commandant. The monument stood in Khartoum commemorating Kitchener's famed conquest of the Sudan but was re-erected in Chatham in 1960 to commemorate his contribution to raising new volunteers during the early days of the First World War. He was killed onboard HMS *Hampshire* whilst en route to Russia on 6 June 1916, when a German submarine sank the ship.

A statue to 'The Conqueror of Canada', Major-General James Wolfe, born at Westerham on 2 January 1727, stands on the village green. Despite his young age, Wolfe was a seasoned soldier, beloved by the people and admired by politicians, royalty and military leaders alike. An army reformer, Wolfe was Britain's most celebrated eighteenth-century military hero. After years of military failure against France, his unlikely victory over them at Quebec in 1759 resulted in Canada's unification with the American colonies under the British crown.

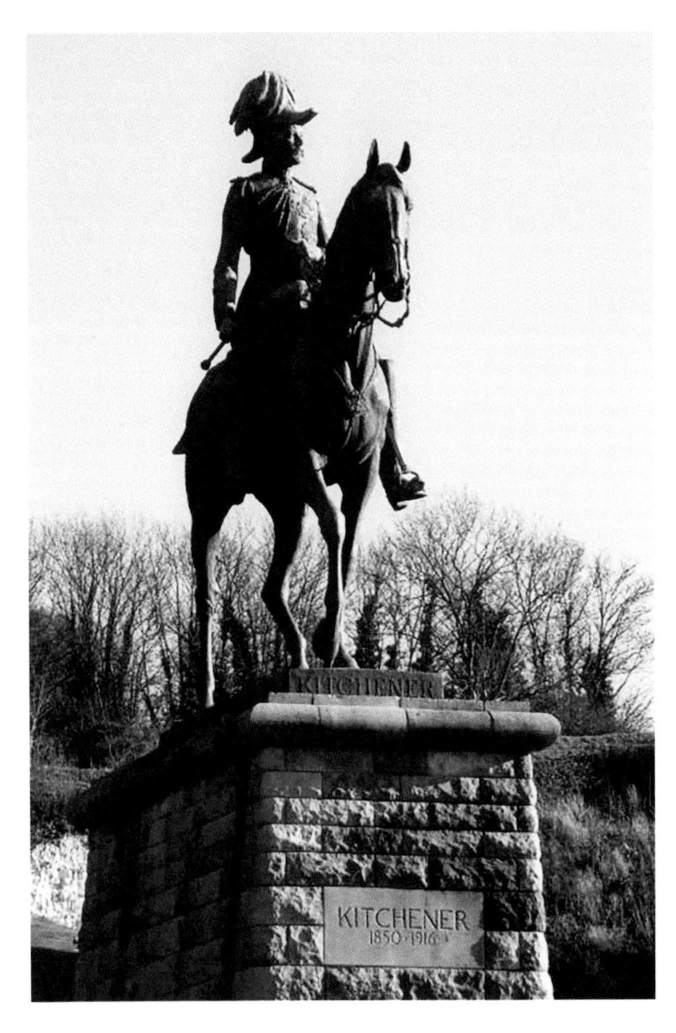

Field Marshal Horatio Kitchener.

Wolfe died leading 4,500 soldiers against a French army on the plains of Abraham during the Battle for Quebec on 13 September 1759. News of his death sparked national grief on a scale unprecedented until the passing of Princess Diana two centuries later. The victory, attributed to his military brilliance, was perceived as a triumph of conservative English beliefs and values over dangerous liberal French ideology. This achievement gave him hero status and a reputation as a patriotic martyr, unrivalled by any Britain until Nelson.

At Capel-le-Ferne between Dover and Folkestone is the 'National Memorial to the Few', a monument to the aircrews and others who gave their lives during the Battle of Britain, from 10 July to 31 October 1940. The site has a large propeller-shaped base; at its centre is the figure of a seated pilot looking out to sea. Behind the monument is a large wall of remembrance containing the names of nearly 3,000 pilots who flew in the battle, and monuments to Air Chief Marshal Sir Keith Park, GCB, KBE, MC & Bar, & DFC, 'The Defender of London'. During 1940 he commanded the RAF's South East and London squadrons during the Battle of Britain. A statue to Bob, the 'Squadron Dog', represents mascots of all Battle of Britain Fighter Command squadrons. The location is served by an interpretation centre that brings to life the victory of 'the Few' over the Luftwaffe.

One of three national naval monuments in the UK, the Chatham Naval Memorial stands above the Historic Dockyard. It commemorates the 8,500 Royal Navy personnel of the First World War and over 10,000 from the second World War who were lost or buried at sea. In the dockyard are many monuments and memorials. Of note is the National

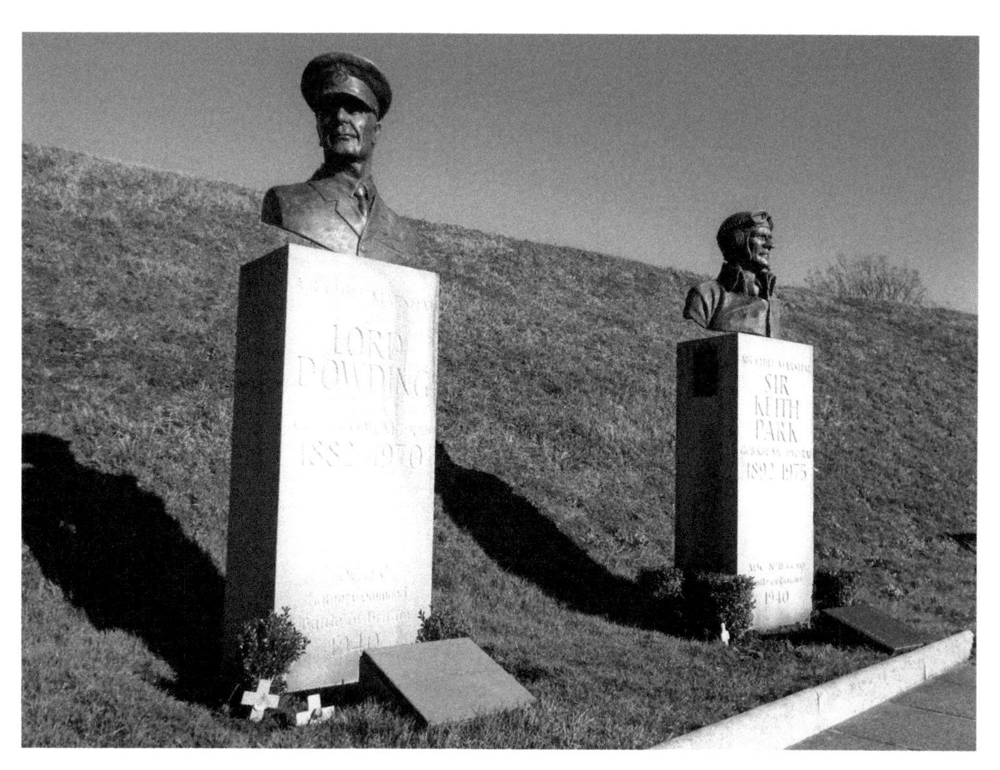

Air Chief Marshal Sir Keith Park.

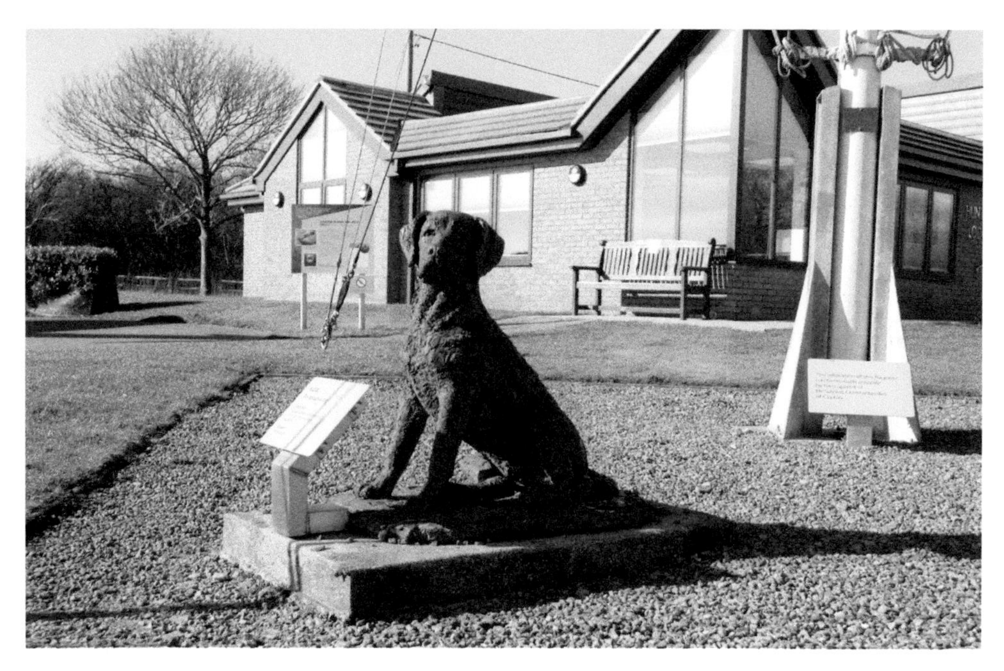

Bob (Battle of Britain) Squadron dog memorial.

Destroyer Memorial, a Second World War Destroyer, HMS *Cavalier*, dedicated to the 139 Royal Navy Destroyers sunk between 1939 and 1945 and nearby the dramatic carved bronze relief of a naval battle dedicated to the 11,000 sailors who lost their lives on those Destroyers during that time.

Memorials

Some memorials are also classified as monuments; others are represented by a variety of objects linked to the memory of an individual or event. An unusual memorial commemorates Second Lieutenant Walter Tull, born in Folkestone in 1888. Tull was killed leading his men into battle in France on the Western Front during the First Battle of Bapaume on 25 March 1918. In 2014 a new road was named after him, Walter Tull Way, near Mundella Primary School, Folkestone, where he'd been a pupil.

Tull was one of several Folkestone men to lose their life in the Great War. So why is he commemorated in this way? Before the war Tull played football for Clapton before turning professional with Tottenham Hotspur and Northampton Town. He signed for Rangers FC but never played for them. As well as this achievement he became the first black infantry officer in the British Army. Following his death, his men made several desperate attempts to recover his body to their trenches, but each failed and he was never recovered.

The Kent Arms at Paddock Wood was teenager John Brunt's local pub before the Second World War. Brunt joined the Queen's Own Royal West Kent Regiment in 1941 as a private and was commissioned into the Sherwood Foresters as a second lieutenant on 2 January 1943. However, he never served with them; instead he followed a friend and joined the 6th Battalion, Lincolnshire Regiment, in North Africa. In September 1943, now a captain in Italy, Brunt received the Military Cross following an engagement with the enemy in which he remained behind to retrieve a wounded comrade.

In December 1944, during a battle with the German 90 Panzer Grenadier Division near Faenza, Brunt showed incredible bravery, repeatedly rescuing men and leading attacks. On one occasion, under fire, he leapt on top of an American Sherman tank and directed fire

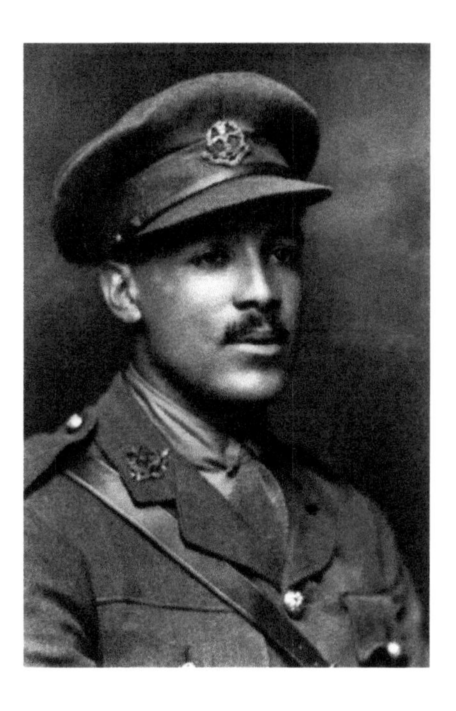

Right: Lieutenant Walter Tull.

Below: Walter Tull road sign.

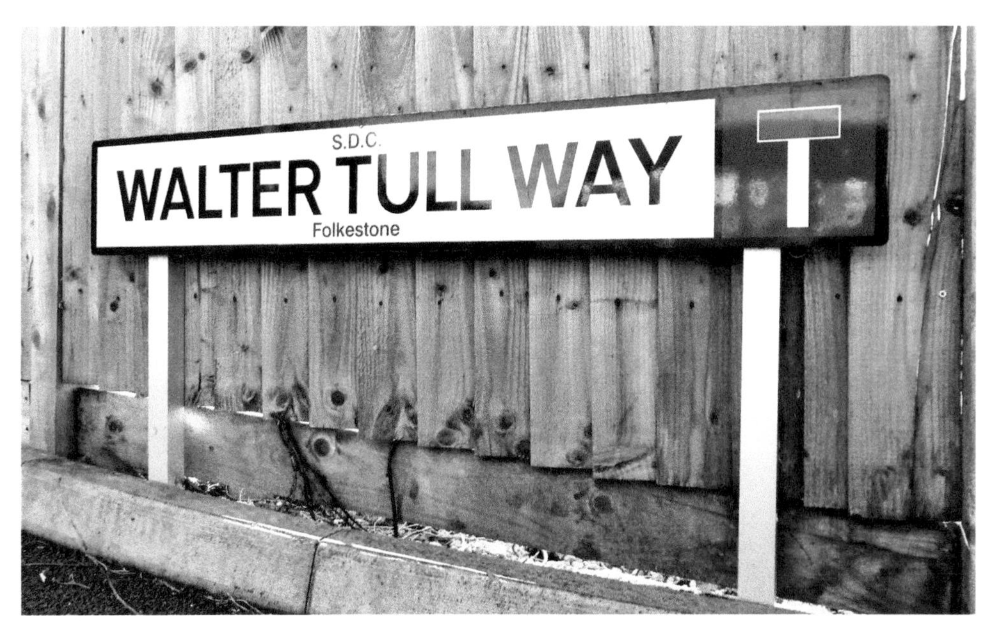

at the enemy. The following day, still only twenty-two, Brunt was killed when a wayward mortar round exploded at his feet while he was drinking tea in the platoon headquarters. For his bravery at Faenza and many other acts, he was posthumously awarded the Victoria Cross. Following the war, locals petitioned Whitbread Brewery to rename the pub after their hero. The brewery agreed and on 3 September 1947 they renamed the pub The John Brunt VC and provided a new pub sign with Brunt's image upon it.

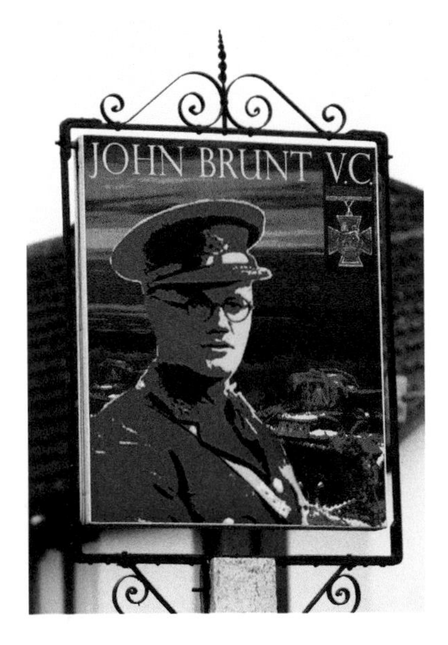

Left: The current John Brunt VC pub sign.

Below: The John Brunt VC public house.

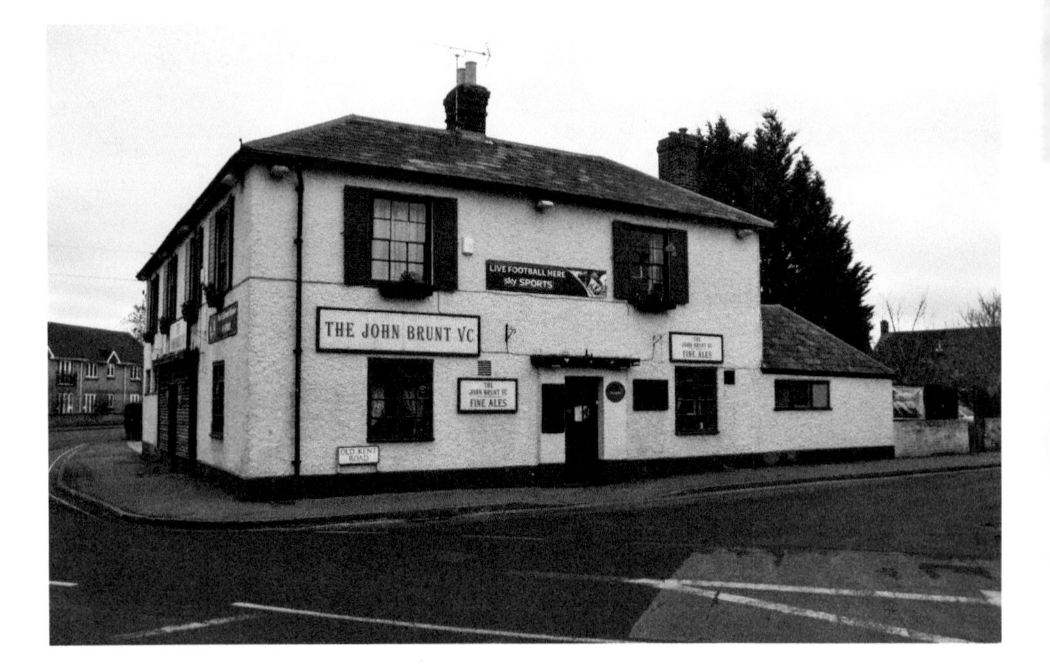

Operation Dynamo, the evacuation of Dunkirk, took place between 26 May and 4 June 1940, resulting in the safe return of 218,226 men of the British Expeditionary Force and 120,000 French and Belgian soldiers. A flotilla of around 800 'Little Ships', civilian vessels of all shapes and sizes, sailed from Dover and Ramsgate. There the navy deployed them to ferry troops from the beaches to the big ships offshore.

At Dover and Ramsgate, memorials pay tribute to the bravery and discipline of the evacuated servicemen, the courage of the crews that rescued them and the people of the ports who received them. Moored in the harbour at Ramsgate is a most unusual memorial, 'The *Sundowner*', one of the original 'Little Ships' that assisted with the evacuation of Dunkirk. Now a museum, it commemorates that event, the 'Little Ships' and the people who sailed them.

Another unusual memorial, a Mark IV tank, number 245, stands in St George's Square, Ashford. The tank acts as a poignant memorial to the pioneers of early mechanical warfare who served and died during the First World War. Presented to the town of Ashford on 1 August 1919 in recognition for its fundraising efforts to the National War Savings appeal during the First World War, it was declared a war memorial in November 2006 and is the only one of its kind to be on public display in a town.

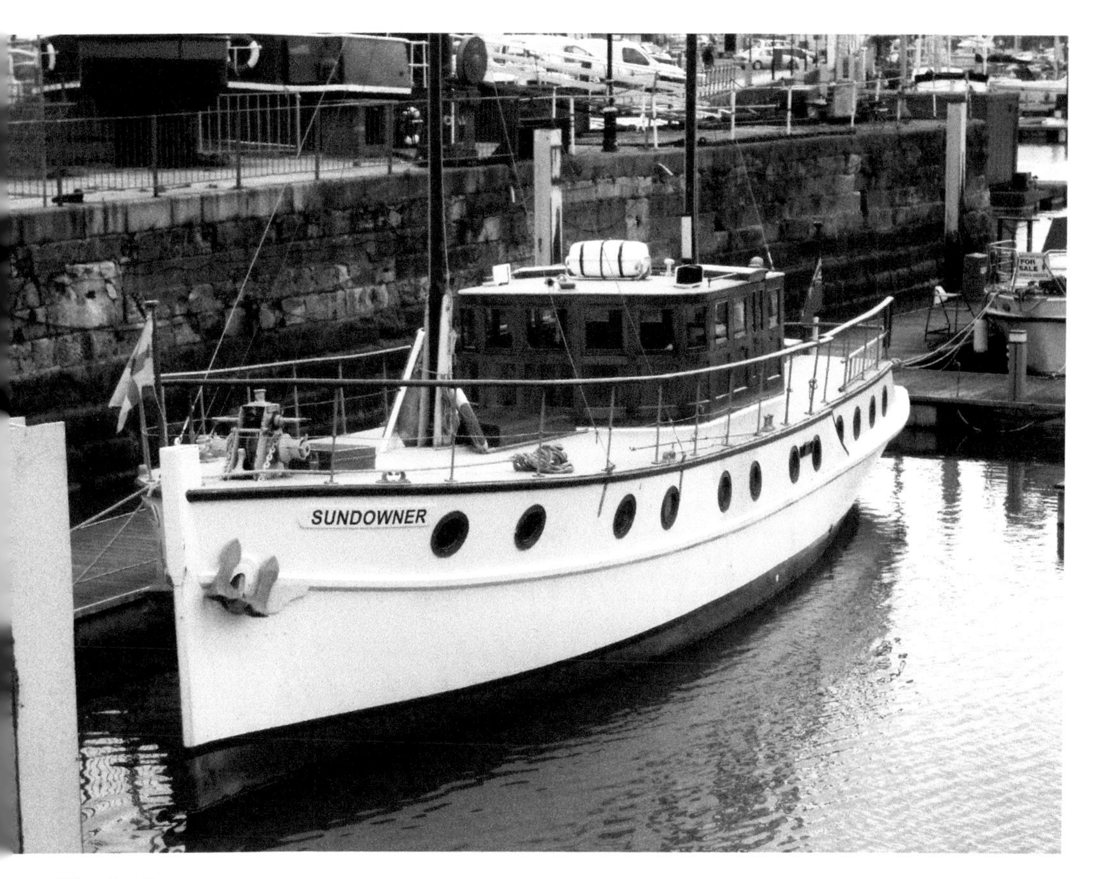

The *Sundowner*.

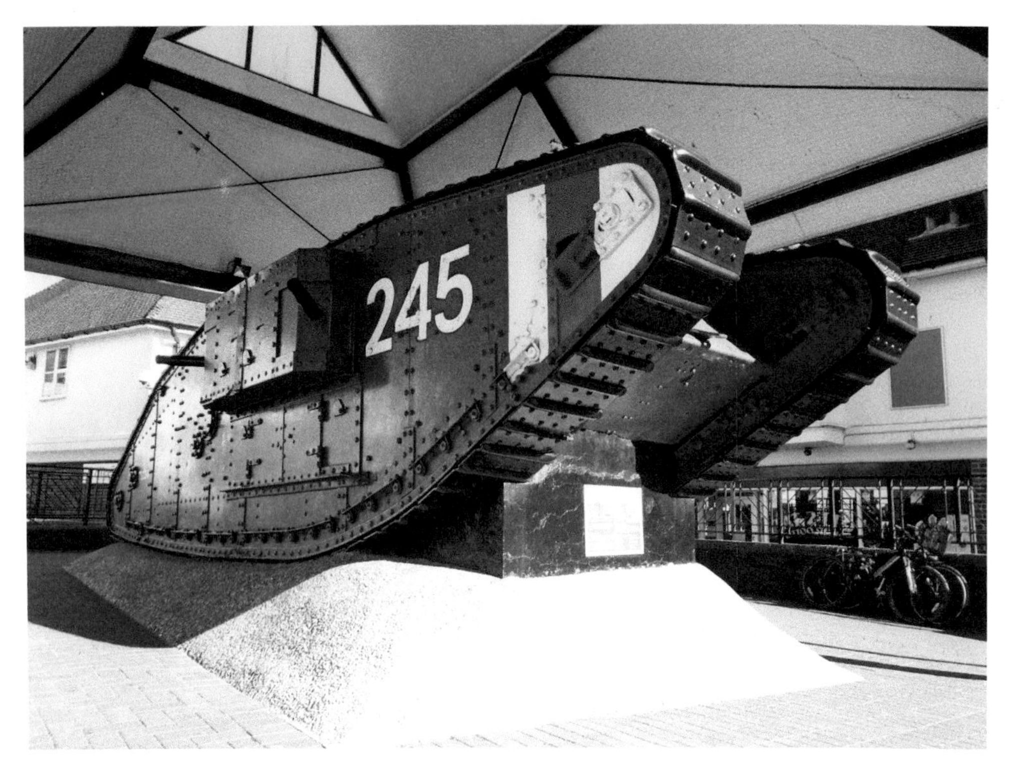

First World War tank, Ashford.

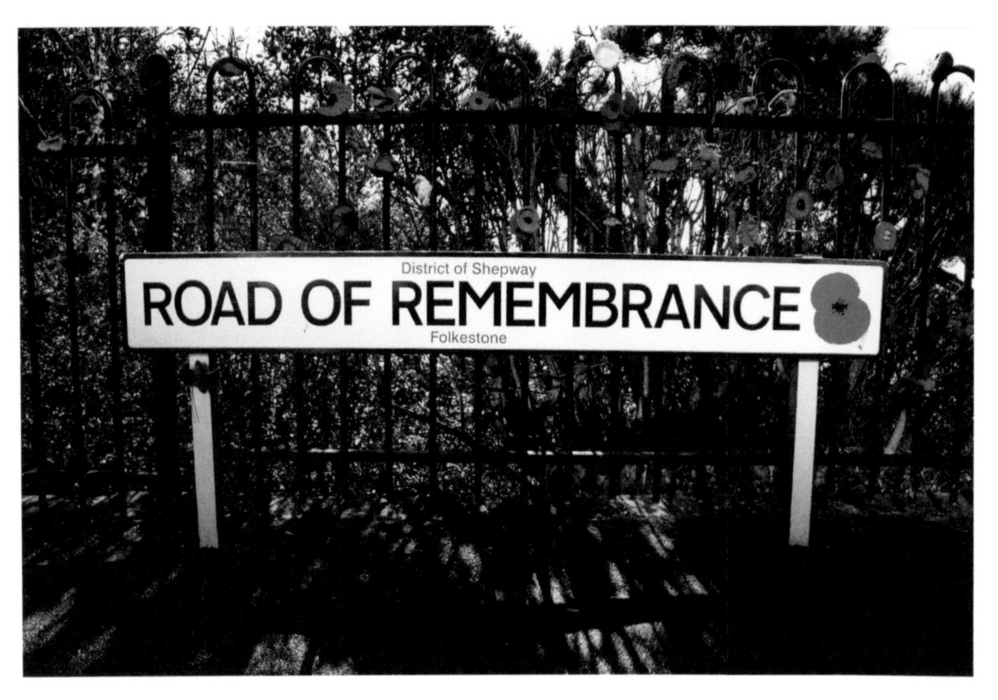

Road of Remembrance road sign.

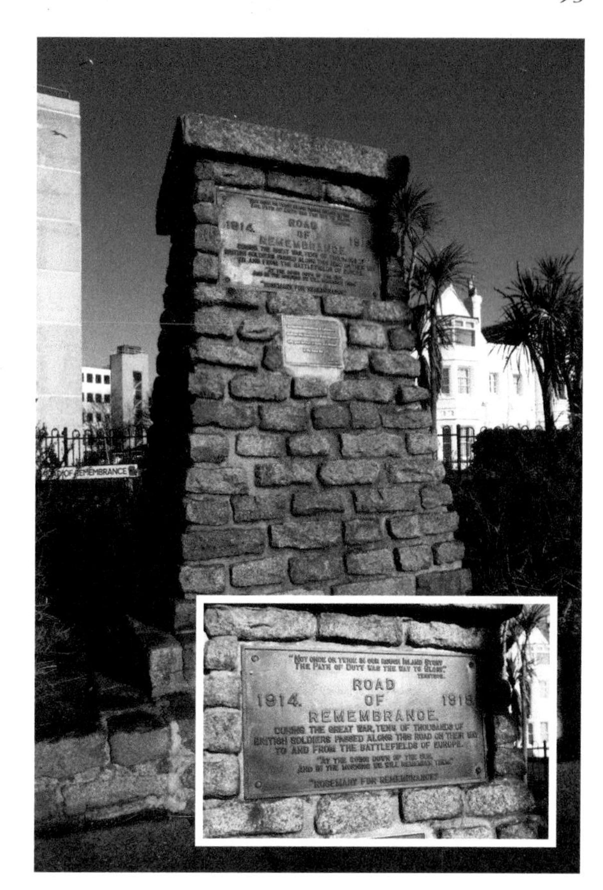

Memorial cairn, Folkestone.

Inset: Bronze plaque on memorial cairn.

Along Folkestone's Road of Remembrance (formally Slope Road, and the final route taken by millions of troops to Folkestone Harbour and embarkation to France and Flanders) are a series of walled plaques that remember them on that journey. Further along the road is a bronze plaque on a cairn memorial, which also marks the bravery of the soldiers who took this route to war, many never to return.

Civic memorials to those who died during the First World War were erected in Deal and Walmer. Additionally, a new hospital was built from public subscriptions as a permanent memorial to the memory of the men of the district who lost their lives. Opened on 17 March 1924 as the Victoria Hospital, it also houses the Roll of Honour for the fallen of Deal and Walmer during the First World War.

Of the many wonderful places of commemoration that can be found in Kent, Folkestone's garden of remembrance uniquely pays tribute to the county's military heritage. Created in 1995, the garden remembers the military and civilian personnel as well as the animals who made and paid the ultimate sacrifice in defence of both county and country. Among the monuments are memorials to those who died in the Holocaust and subsequent memorials, the recipients of six Victoria Crosses, the Ghurkhas killed in Afghanistan, the victims of the Tontine air raid and to those animals who have served in war and peace.

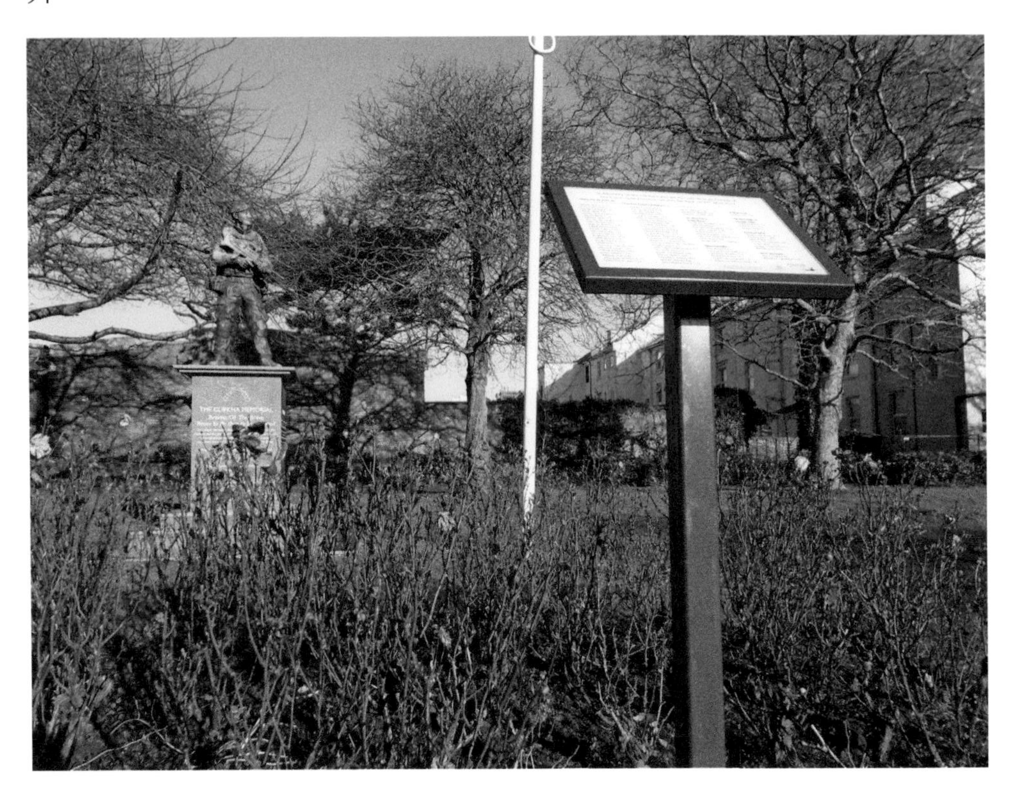

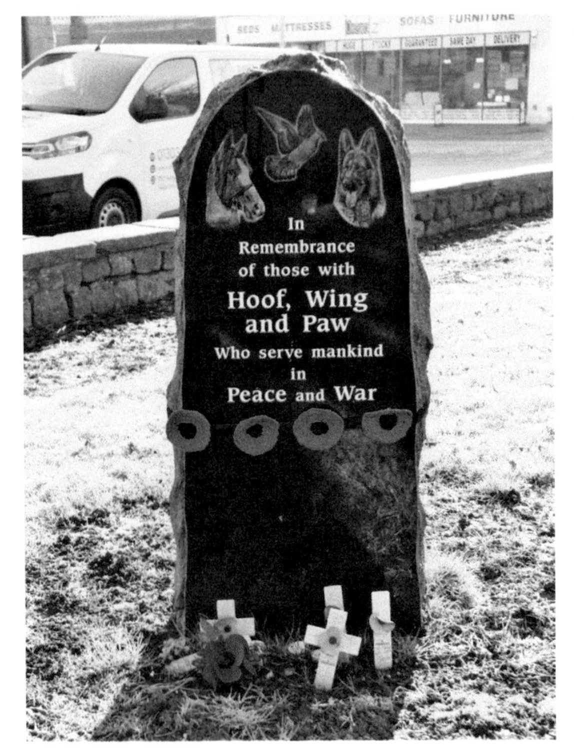

Above: Gurkha and Tontine Street memorials.

Left: Memorial to hoof, wing and paw.

Acknowledgements

In finding the primary sources needed to research the subject of this publication I am thankful to the many wonderful and like-minded people I have met along the way. Their help, guidance and support have proved invaluable. I am thankful to the staff of the Kent History and Library Centre, Chatham Historic Dockyard, Deal Castle, Deal Maritime and Local History Museum, Dover Castle, Dover Museum, The Kent and Sharpshooters Yeomanry Museum, The Kent Battle of Britain Museum, The Queen's Own Royal West Kent Regiment Museum, The National Army Museum, and Rushmoor Writers, without whose knowledge, guidance and support it would not have been possible to complete this project.

Images: I am obliged to Dave Robinson, Aviation Ancestry at https://www.aviationancestry.co.uk, Peter Schute (PS), Pillbox Study Group (PSG) at www.pillbox-study-group.org.uk, Ian Capper (IC.), Steve Popple (SP.), Piers Pardoe (PP.) and Dreamstime (DT.). All other images are from the author's collection.

I offer special thanks for their continued meritorious support of me and their kindness in helping to bring this project to life, for which I am eternally grateful: my wife, Maria Hollands, good friend Catherine Milne, and fellow authors Sharon Berry and Christopher Berry. I am also grateful to Amberley for their continued support and for making my ambitions a reality and Dave Brocklehurst MBE of the Battle of Britain Museum.

About the Author

Dean Hollands comes from a military family and his interest in military history spans over four decades. Having served eight years with the Royal Army Ordnance Corps as a Supply Specialist and Physical Training Instructor in the UK, West Germany and the Falkland Islands, Dean served with Surrey Police for twenty-six years.

Now retired, Dean spends much of his time conducting battlefield tours in the UK and Europe, giving talks, undertaking research, and writing about his interests. He has regularly visited the USA to talk at the New Jersey State Association of Chiefs of Police's Senior Leadership Programme and annually delivers bespoke leadership training for the NJSACOP's European battlefield staff ride programme.

Dean is the Chair of the Friends of Aldershot Military Museum, where he is also a volunteer guide for the Commonwealth War Graves Commission, is a member of the Battlefield Trust, Guild of Battlefield Guides, Western Front Association, Aldershot Militaria Society, and regularly appears as a guest on the British Forces Broadcasting Service's Garrison FM radio at Aldershot.

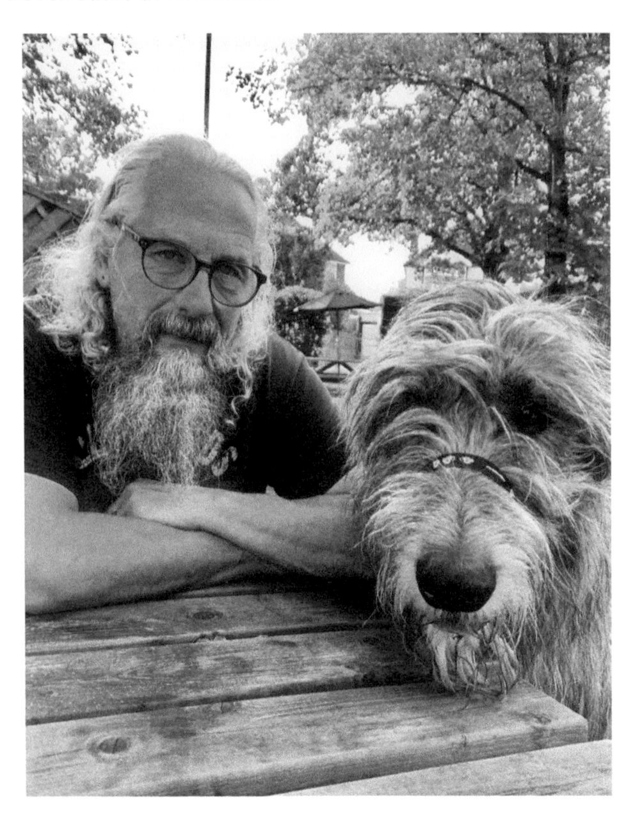